NELL McCAFFERTY was born in Bogside, Derry city, Northern Ireland in 1944. After completing a B.A. degree at Queen's University, Belfast, she became involved with the civil rights and Irish women's movements. Now a renowned freelance journalist and television and radio commentator, she lives in Dublin. Her writings have been collected in *The Best of Nell* (1983) and *Goodnight Sisters* (1987). She has also written a powerful investigative study, *A Woman to Blame: The Kerry Babies Case* (1985) and her first play, *The Worm in the Heart* (1987) was performed in Dublin and London.

Hailed by the Irish *Sunday Tribune* as 'a singular voice in Irish society', Nell McCafferty is also described by the *Irish Press* as 'an original . . . one of those few lucky people that must be loved or hated, because she has a magnetic pull that polarises energy . . . she's a bloody good journalist'.

In *Peggy Deery*, Nell McCafferty takes us to the heart of the trouble in Northern Ireland by focusing on the true life story of a Derry woman and her fourteen children. Unlike any other book, this one brings home what family life on the front line is really like. *Peggy Deery* does not present an impartial view; it is an important insider's view that goes far beyond our television news.

'*Peggy Deery* is a testimony to all the Peggy Deerys in this unjust world who nurture, and protect and love their families and whose entire lives are spent making elbow room for them at the bottom of the pile'
– Bernadette McAliskey, *The Irish Times*

For *Mary Nelis*, who says that the last twenty years in Derry have changed all our lives for the better, despite the worst.

PEGGY DEERY

DEERY

A Derry Family at War

Nell McCafferty

Published by VIRAGO PRESS Limited 1989
20–23 Mandela Street, Camden Town, London NW1 0HQ

First published in Ireland by Attic Press, 1988

*A CIP Catalogue record for this book
is available from the British Library*

Printed in Great Britain by
Cox & Wyman Ltd, Reading, Berkshire

Contents

FAMILY TREE

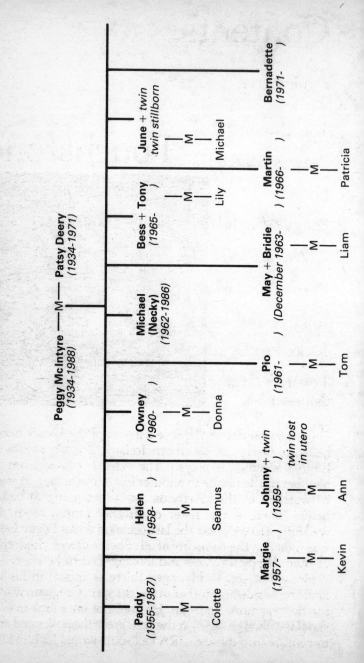

Peggy McIntyre ——M—— **Patsy Deery**
(1934-1988)   *(1934-1971)*

Paddy
(1955-1987)
—M—
Colette

Margie
(1957-)
—M—
Kevin

Helen
(1958-)
—M—
Seamus

Johnny + *twin*
(1959-) *twin lost in utero*
—M—
Ann

Owney
(1960-)
—M—
Donna

Pio
(1961-)
—M—
Tom

Michael (Necky)
(1962-1986)

May + **Bridie**
(December 1963-)
—M—
Liam

Bess + **Tony**
(1965-)
—M—
Lily

Martin
(1966-)
—M—
Patricia

June + *twin*
twin stillborn
—M—
Michael

Bernadette
(1971-)

Touchstone

The Deery Family

On any given day of the week, in one of the Deery house-
holds in Derry, in Northern Ireland, a video of Owney
Deery's wedding is played. The video is passed from one
member of the family to another like a touchstone. It might
be watched in the afternoon, or before going to bed, or
before dawn, if the sister or brother cannot sleep. The
wedding, in 1985, was the last occasion when Peggy Deery
was filmed in the company of all of her fourteen children, all
of them happy and well and looking glad to be alive.

Her eldest son Paddy, aged thirty, is shown in his suit,
kneeling beside his mother in the chapel in Creggan, waiting
for the ceremony to begin. He does not once look over his
shoulder, though he is on the run. Were the police and army
to venture into the area, IRA look-outs would let him know

soon enough. Peggy, in a black trouser-suit, with white shirt and black string tie, pearl earrings and a red carnation in her lapel, is clearly delighted with Paddy's company.

Owney, in formal morning suit, on his wedding day, has the looks of a young Clark Gable, complete with dimples, pencil moustache and cleft chin. He holds the hand of his bride, Donna, as they sit in chairs before the altar watching the priest say mass. A choir of schoolchildren sings the song which the couple have chosen specially for their wedding. They sing 'The Rose', with which Bette Midler had a hit record.

The video shows Peggy later, at the reception in a singing pub, dancing with her son Tony. He is far too tall for her, and she must rest her head upon his chest, as they move slowly, waltzing badly, to the music of a band which is playing 'When the evening shadows fall'.

Michael interrupts them, making everybody laugh as he prances about in a bra, and skirt and boots. Martin and Johnny and Owney dance with their mother in turn. Her eight daughters come onto the floor, and all the guests, and they form a circle, kicking their legs up as the tempo increases. Peggy moves awkwardly, her left leg dragging, but she beams constantly.

When the band takes a break, a guest takes the microphone and sings a song which he has composed himself. He is not from Derry. He sings a lament for a dead IRA hunger-striker. His audience pays him no attention at all.

The video ends with everybody being asked what they wish for the married couple. Peggy looks into the camera and hesitates and then she says, simply and seriously, 'I just hope everything goes well for them.'

Owney studies this video constantly. He and Donna often talk late into the night about how their own family will turn out. They look forward to more babies. Donna says you get too much enjoyment out of children ever to complain about them. The video reassures Owney that Peggy Deery, on her best days, had no complaints about the fourteen childrei who danced around her.

Peggy's March

Peggy

It used to be that there was only one thing for a Catholic mother to do in Derry on a fine, wintry, Sunday afternoon. On rare occasions her man would come with her, but usually she would go with another woman, a sister or sister-in-law, or once in a while, a female neighbour. The women would bring their children with them.

These Sunday afternoons, spent strolling in the city cemetery were a comparative treat. The alternative for mothers was to sit at home, for the seventh day in a row, in the strict and doleful grip of a Protestant Sabbath. In Northern Ireland, on a Sunday, it used to be that everything closed down – no playgrounds, no cinemas, no pubs, no shops, nothing but the lonely toll of church bells even after the churches had closed.

The cemetery was, by contrast, a bazaar. Magnificently situated on a hill overlooking Derry, with views of the River Foyle that bisects the town, and the mountains marching towards the Republic of Ireland beyond, it afforded a sense of beauty, freedom, and reward, if not in this life, then in the next. In the cemetery, the minds and tongues of women at leisure were free to wander. The inscribed tombstones among which children played hide-and-seek were a rich source of gossip, speculation and tribal perspective. The people of the town, which had a small population of 65,000, were intimately acquainted with each other, and with each other's seed, breed and generation.

The launching of the Civil Rights Movement in Derry, in 1968, changed dramatically the nature of Sunday afternoons. The movement liberated Catholic women, albeit unintentionally. They burst out of their homes, and out of the cemetery, and spent their Sundays marching around the city, demanding freedom, just like the men and children. They joined in the chant for votes, houses and jobs, carried banners, sat down defiantly in the roadway when the Royal Ulster Constabulary blocked the route, helped build barricades, inhaled tear gas, broke the law for the first time in their adult lives and agreed that there was no time to go home to make the supper.

The marches frequently deteriorated into routine set-piece battles between Derry teenagers on one hand and police and British soldiers on the other. On such Sunday afternoons, adults settled themselves into spectator positions on the hills, and watched the riots.

Hardly anybody died.

In the years between 1968 and 1972, violent death in Derry was a rare and confusing occurrence, and when someone was killed one side would protest, the other would bluster, and there was a general insistence that it was not meant to happen. This was a struggle for civil rights, not a war. People were so confident of this that they continued to march on Sundays.

*

Peggy Deery put on her best clothes for her last march. The 38-year-old widow, mother of fourteen children, dressed herself in a black mock-leather wet-look coat, which had black fun-fur trimming at the hem, and wore black wet-look boots. She left her eldest daughter Margie, aged fourteen, in charge of the house.

The march began at the top of Derry's highest hill, where the Creggan housing estate in which Peggy lived was situated. She left her home, a prefabricated one-storey aluminium bungalow and walked the short distance to the dilapidated playing field where thousands of people had gathered. She joined her nieces there, Rita and Sandra.

There was a band playing. The weather was unseasonally fine, hinting of spring. People were in good humour. The proposed route would take them on a bracing three-mile walk, downhill all the way, skirting the cemetery to plunge into Brandywell below, then back along the valley of the Bogside, and if possible, out of these Catholic ghettos into the city centre.

The victories so far achieved gave a feeling of confidence on this day. The corrupt Unionist-controlled corporation had been abolished. The provincial Unionist Government at Stormont had been pressurised to build houses for Catholics in Derry. The Unionist minister for home affairs, William Craig, *bête noire* of the Catholics and champion of the mainly Protestant police force, had been dismissed. There had been a price to pay – the internment without trial of hundreds of Catholic males – but even that ploy had rebounded. International opinion was ranged against internment, especially when it emerged that the only thing the internees had in common was the private practice of their religion or a commitment to civil rights. There was scarcely an IRA man among them.

Peggy and Rita and Sandra had a very enjoyable march. They sang all the way. When the marchers moved out beyond the barricades in Rossville Street, out of the Bogside and into the bottleneck of William Street, the police and army were waiting. A huge military tanker released a jet of coloured water onto their heads. The dye would help snatch-squads sort out civilians from civil-rights activists should anyone penetrate to the centre of town. Stones were thrown at the troops, in retaliation. Young people pushed forward, older people tried to retreat.

In the roaring confusion, in the narrow canyon created by the houses and shops on either side of William Street, Rita chose the only escape from the crush. She climbed a lamp-post, grabbed hold of the bulb, and hung on. Sandra and her aunt Peggy laughed at her. They could not persuade her to come down. They left her to take her chances while they pushed their way back through the crowd, round the corner and into Rossville Street. 'I'm away on now,' were Peggy's parting words to Sandra. 'I have to take a wee cake up to your granny.' Peggy had brought a home-baked scone on the march, which she intended to deliver to her mother in the Bogside.

When the crowd thinned out, Rita got down off the lamp-post. She did not go back towards Rossville Street. She went forward towards the troops, into the no-man's land between soldiers and rioters. The established ritual of riot procedure allowed for a cessation in hostilities if a woman wished to get through the lines. The cessation would be brief, a few seconds, and the woman would have to run quickly. On occasion, there would be no lull at all, but rioters would take care to throw stones over her head, and soldiers and police would not aim rubber bullets at her.

There was no lull this day but there was safety in the number of adults who ran forward in order to escape. So Rita ran forward and turned into Chamberlain Street. She could hear in the distance the amplified voice of Bernadette Devlin addressing the civil rights meeting. As she ran down the street, soldiers of the First Battalion of the Parachute Regiment, Britain's crack army unit, ran after her. 'There were bullets hitting off the walls, and a man was pulling me along and then I was standing in some woman's doorway. She said it was only rubber bullets, and we stood there listening, and then everything went quiet.'

The soldiers had run down Rossville Street also, towards the meeting. Peggy saw them coming and she ran through the courtyard of a nearby block of flats, heading for the presumed safety of Chamberlain Street. A bullet struck her in the back of her left leg. She called out to a fleeing priest: 'Father, I think I'm shot,' and he called out: 'Keep on running,' and she did, and then she collapsed on the step of a back door of a Chamberlain Street house. As she lay on the ground a soldier with red hair came alongside. She looked up at him and said she was the mother of fourteen children. He ran on. People ran over her as she lay there. She felt their shoes strike and hurt her head. Her wounded leg felt cold. A man pulled her down an alleyway and in the front door of a house in Chamberlain Street.

It was from television newscasts that Rita got the number to phone for information on dead, injured or missing relatives. She went with her father, hours later, to Altnagelvin Hospital, to look for Peggy. In the upper floors, people crowded outside operating rooms. A doctor confirmed the rumour that Peggy had indeed been wounded, but could give no details. Confusion abounded. Rita went to the ground floor to get cigarettes from a vending machine. 'The ground floor was empty. There was nobody there. The whole place was dead quiet, no people, nothing.' A man appeared, clad in a white coat and white hat. She could see his clerical collar. 'He asked me if I had anybody in the hospital. I said, "What do you want to know for?" I didn't know the difference between a Protestant minister and a priest, or he might have been an army chaplain. He said his name was Fr Tom O'Gara. He said the morgue was on the ground floor. He said there were thirteen dead people in there. He asked me if I would go in and see if I could identify anybody. I said no way. Then the whole McDaid family arrived. He took them to the morgue. I can hear them squealing yet.'

Upstairs, doctors operated on the twenty-eight wounded.

Later that night, as Rita and her father left the hospital, they saw policemen on the ground floor. 'Two of the cops were singing "It's a Beautiful Day". That was the first time in my life I ever cursed in front of my father.

The Civil Rights Movement died in Derry, on Bloody Sunday, 30 January 1972. Henceforth, when people regained the nerve to march, they marched increasingly behind the banner of Sinn Féin, political wing of the IRA.

*

The bullet severed the sciatic nerve on Peggy's upper thigh. Half of the buttock had been shot away. There was no sensation in her foot. It seemed as if gangrene was inevitable. Surgeons arranged to amputate her leg on Wednesday morning.

On Tuesday night Peggy's body reacted to the four pints of blood which had been hastily transfused into her on Bloody Sunday. In the consternation and chaos of mass operations there had been no time to cross-match blood samples, and she had been given rhesus positive. She was rhesus negative. Acute kidney failure threatened. 'It was as serious as could be. Her life was in the balance,' says her general practitioner Dr Donal McDermott, who was informed by the hospital of the crisis. Peggy was transferred through the night to a specialist unit in Belfast. She was jaundiced and unconscious. She spent eight weeks there. When she returned to Altnagelvin Hospital, Dr McDermott went to see her. Peggy said to him: 'I can move my big toe.' He told her this was medically impossible. That a severed nerve does not grow again, and five inches of the nerve had been shot away. Nevertheless, Peggy could move her toe.

'Had she been given the right transfusion at the start, her leg would have been amputated as scheduled. She was lucky the soldiers shot so many people.' Dr McDermott has a jaundiced view of British soldiers. His son joined the IRA after Bloody Sunday and is now serving a life sentence in jail.

*

On the night she was shot Peggy Deery's children were looked after by Fr Tom O'Gara. The 25-year-old stranger, who had long hair and a guitar, walked into their home with loads of buns and chips. He made them eat and ate with them and Margie was affronted when one of the children knocked the priest's fork to the floor. She rose to get a tea-cloth but he wiped the fork on his trousers saying there was no need. Then he played his guitar and sang for them. He sang 'Ebony Eyes' and 'Dirty Old Town'. He helped Margie wash the younger ones and put them to bed. It took Margie a while to realise that this man was not a plain-clothes British soldier, sent to keep an eye on them while their mother was, as she thought, being questioned and arrested in hospital. Fr O'Gara told Margie that he had been specially seconded by his bishop to look after the Deery family.

*

A group of concerned priests gathered together the day after Bloody Sunday to decide on a collective response. The then bishop, Neil Farren, was not at the meeting. An elderly arch-conservative, he was bemuddled and swamped by the tide of history and he retreated into his palace demesne. The fifteen priests relived the events of the previous day, which many of them had personally witnessed. They assured themselves of two things. The soldiers were the only ones who had fired shots during the massacre, and all of the victims were unarmed. Fr O'Gara mentioned that he had seen two armed members of the IRA, in the vicinity of the slaughter, about ten minutes before the soldiers swept into the Bogside. This fact was not included in the press state-ment which the priests then issued. They confined their des-cription of events to the beginning, duration and end of the soldiers' onslaught; no one who died or had been shot was a member of the IRA; no shots were fired at the soldiers; the dead and injured were unarmed.

The British Army also issued statements. All of the dead were in possession of guns or nail-bombs, and nail-bombs had been found in the pockets of their clothing. The British Information Service telegraphed embassies abroad that four of the dead were on the RUC wanted-list.

A public inquiry, instituted by the British Government, subsequently found that none of the dead were in possession of anything other than the undigested remains of their dinners, 'meat, peas and potatoes', in the graphic words of Dr Raymond McClean, who represented the Catholic Church at the post mortems.

Everything that the priests had said in their statement was true and everything that the British Army and British Information Service had said in theirs was untrue. Nevertheless, Fr O'Gara's information, had it been divulged, would have been a propaganda godsend to the British Government in the immediate aftermath of Bloody Sunday.

The relationship between the Catholic Church and its people, and the attitude of the Catholic Church to government authorities in the North, since this war began, has been delicate and fraught with ambiguity. Fr O'Gara was only one of hundreds of priests who found themselves torn as the war deepened. In a document which he drew up and circulated to the clergy he outlined his view of the ministry. The document presaged the moral disarray into which Derry would eventually fall, because of the war. The Church, he wrote, did not appreciate the level or depth of people's insecurities.

> We miss the insecurities that riddle so much of their thinking ... These insecurities are practical needs and must determine enormously the shape into which a man's heart might be pushed and can be constrained ... is it the insecurity brought by the fear of having no money to pay for family needs etc. which drives people to cheat, draw false dole, drink and even kill? ... I cannot answer for certain whether the people living in estates feel their lives empty. I must know more of this.

Fr O'Gara knew the Deery family better than any other priest. He spent years with them, married, baptised and counselled many of them and their relatives. He died young. Peggy continued with confidence to summon the clergy to attend all the great family rituals of birth and death and army raids and police arrests. She felt no insecurity whatsoever about her personal relationship with God.

Bogside

Women relaxing in the sun in Bogside

The poet Seamus Deane, describing the area in which he was born and reared, wrote: 'Bogside was once a street. Now it is a condition.' The condition was one of poor housing, low pay and unemployment in the swampy valley below the walled city of Derry. Bogside was the name of the main street in the swamp. The population there was and is almost exclusively Catholic.

The condition known as 'Bogside' is indelibly imprinted in the memories of those who rose up against it in 1968, pouring out of the warrens that surrounded the main street. The names of these other streets, in which the people lived in tenements, evoke pride in those who once dwelt there. The streets are gone now, replaced by modern housing in response to the Civil Rights Movement. The former slum-dwellers are proud that they survived and overcame the worst that the Unionist Government inflicted on them.

Those streets which best evoked the condition known as 'Bogside' were called Fahan Street, Walker's Square, Nailor's Row, and St Columb's Wells. The condition was not confined to the Bogside area. It was to be found wherever Catholics sought shelter. Within the walled city, it was to be found in Magazine Street; abutting the walled city it was to be found in Bridge Street and an alleyway off it called Miller's Close; beyond the city boundary it was to be found, notoriously, in Springtown Camp.

Peggy Deery's parents were born in these streets. The parents of her husband Patsy were born in these streets. The parents reared their children in these streets. Peggy and Patsy began their marriage in a rented room in one of these streets.

*

Peggy's father, John McIntyre, was born in Bridge Street. He moved with his wife Maggie into nearby Miller's Close, separated from Bridge Street by a pub called 'Buckets of Blood'. The area was the scene of regular armed confrontation during the bloody years of the birth of the sundered North in the twenties.

After a series of moves forced by overcrowding the family finally settled into a newly built private house in Limewood Street in the heart of the Bogside, where the fifth and last child Peggy was born in 1933. Their fortunes had improved dramatically, thanks to the regular wages which John McIntyre and his two sons earned as soldiers in the British Army.

Until 1968, enrolment in the British Armed Services had been a paradoxical safety valve for the unemployed. Service to the Crown was regarded by the Unionist Government as a mark in favour of the Catholic male subject, in consequence of which he was given preferential treatment on the rare occasion when a Catholic was considered for a government job, such as postman. The unwritten code was applied by foreign business people when they located government-sponsored factories in the North.

All the men of the McIntyre family fought in British uniform in the Second World War, and all survived, albeit in varying degrees of bad health. Peggy's brother John spent D-day in the water after his troop-ship was sunk. Her brother Charlie was a prisoner of war in Burma.

After the Second World War, while Peggy was a dancing teenager, her father and two elder brothers and her older sister Nellie and Nellie's husband found regular summer employment in a Butlin's holiday camp in England. Nellie remembers vividly the one singular pleasure of those years. 'Every Wednesday, from April to September, we'd telegram home five pay packets to my mammy and Peggy.'

In winter, the men took what casual work was available in Derry, and Nellie and Peggie worked in the shirt factories, the staple local industry for women. The family income was supplemented by the mother, Maggie, who was famous in the Bogside for her toffee apples. She boiled up vats of toffee in her kitchen, dipped the apples into them, and left the delicious confections to dry on a tray that poked appetisingly out of the front window of her house. Queues used form on a Friday night outside Maggie McIntyre's house as children arrived to spend their pocket-money. Out of season, she sold toffee squares in wax paper. The kitchen was regularly examined by a government health-inspector, anxious to ensure that the Catholic subjects of Her Majesty were eating only the very best fast food.

Maggie also tried to augment income by a daily gamble on the horses. Her grandchildren were a familiar local sight, betting slip and coins in hand, as they trotted a well-worn path between her home and the betting shop, which was located in a back lane. It was Maggie's money which paid for headstones for those babies born dead to her daughter Nellie, who had seventeen miscarriages and still-births as well as five children.

*

Peggy's husband Patsy Deery had an even more hardy rearing. His family came out of Walker's Square, site of the most legendary tenements in the history of the city of Derry. The square abutted onto, and below, the city walls. Above the huddled Catholics, and planted firmly onto the ramparts, was a vast pillar and atop that was a statue of Governor Walker, the Protestant who defended the city against the siege of the English Catholic King James in 1690. Governor Walker was fighting for representative democracy, an ideal which became lost in the mists of time in the North. Once a year, until the IRA blew up the statue in 1973, members of the Protestant Orange Order used gather under the pillar and throw pennies to the Catholics below. Catholic children such as Patsy Deery grew up gladly gathering those pennies. He was one of ten sisters and brothers. Surviving members of his family remember that one room of their small tenement in Walker's Square was in such dangerous condition that the children were forbidden to enter it, lest they crash through the ceiling.

After the Second World War, when the Allies pulled out of emergency billets in Derry, the more desperate of the citizenry squatted into the abandoned camps. Patsy Deery's family went first to the British Army nissen huts on the outskirts of town. A reconnoitre of the area later showed that Springtown Camp was a slightly better proposition. The American Army had erected Springtown, and the Yanks were known to appreciate luxury.

Hundreds of Catholics, including the Deerys, and some Protestants, swarmed into Springtown Camp. There was no electricity in the tin huts; there was no indoor water supply; the people used two communal taps and a communal latrine; some families shared a hut, marking the division of property with a curtain.

Springtown Camp was an improvement on their condition.

The Ministry of Health and Local Government for Northern Ireland made the squatters sign a licence in order to become legal tenants. The licence declared that:

the occupier will use the premises for residential purposes only and will not carry on or permit to be carried on therein any trade or business and will not do, or permit to be done, any act or thing which may cause discomfort or annoyance to other occupiers of the said premises ... and will at all times during his or her occupation keep the said premises in a clean state and condition.

Springtown Camp did not close until 1968.

*

Peggy and Patsy had left Derry long before that. Shortly after their wedding they went to Portsmouth, the great naval town in England, where one of Peggy's sisters, May, had made a comfortable home. Patsy worked as a painter alongside his brother Mickey. They could have found work twenty-four hours a day, says Mickey, painting navy ships. Peggy worked in a bleach factory. Within a year of arrival she gave birth to her first child, Paddy. It was the feelings they had of being outsiders in England on the day of Paddy's birth which made them decide to return to Derry, his parents were later to say.

Paddy Deery was born on Poppy Day, on 11 November 1955. Poppy Day is of immense significance to the British. On that date, throughout the United Kingdom, the people gather at war memorials in city, town and village to commemorate the dead of both World Wars. Neither his parents, nor Paddy in his time, ever took part in such commemorations. They felt themselves to be part of an excluded minority, the Irish in Britain, and part of an excluded minority, the Catholic Irish in Northern Ireland. Peggy was also to admit that she missed her mother. There was no extended family network of grannies and aunts in Portsmouth.

Upon return to Derry, Peggy and Patsy lived with Peggy's parents. When their family increased they moved to tenement rooms in Magazine Street. Patsy's brother Buddy lived with his wife and children in the rooms below. Buddy remembers calling up to Patsy for a cigarette, and Patsy pushing the cigarette down through a crack in the floor-boards. A neighbour remembers sheltering Peggy and her growing brood after a marital squabble. Unemployment and multiple births and slum dwelling had begun to take their toll.

There was a cancer in the marriage as surely as there was cancer in her young husband's body by the time the family obtained a council house in Creggan. To qualify for council housing, a Catholic family had to be very large and quite sick. Peggy Deery had thirteen children, and a dying husband, before she found herself settled into a home that had its own bathroom, own front door, and own grass patch, in Swilly Gardens. Her condition was one of absolute poverty. She joined the Civil Rights Movement. She gave birth to her last and fourteenth child. She named the girl Bernadette Devlin Deery, after the civil rights leader. The naming was an act of hope and defiance by a woman reborn.

Peggy's Birthday

Paddy

Six months after Bloody Sunday, British soldiers blinded Peggy's son Paddy, in one eye, in the most casual way. He was on his way to the city centre to buy a sports jacket. The money for the jacket was a gift from his mother, who was celebrating her thirty-ninth birthday. Strangers were still sending her cash gifts, and Peggy's way of celebrating was to give presents to all her children. The route to the shops took Paddy straight into a protest, staged outside the Bogside Inn, and he stopped to watch.

It was a fine summer afternoon, 9 August 1972, and the demonstration was staged with the flair and panache now customary among seasoned campaigners. Bogsiders were still mesmerised by the political drama in which they were cast centre-stage, and they never tired of watching themselves act and re-enact the parts for which they had been chosen. Derry, said American journalist Jimmy Breslin at the time, was the only place in the world where people ran towards the sound of gunfire.

On this day, Peggy's birthday, the demonstrators were re-enacting the events of exactly one year ago, 9 August 1971, when internment without trial had been introduced. A mock internment camp was set up, into which people pretending to be British soldiers enthusiastically beat yelling people who pretended to be internees. The 'internees' were spreadeagled against the wall of the Bogside Inn, and the 'soldiers' subjected them to a facsimile of internment-camp procedure. The actual procedure was condemned, subsequently, by the European Court of Justice, as 'cruel and unusual'.

The demonstration recalled to the onlookers, of whom Paddy was one, exactly what had happened. Hundreds of Catholic males throughout the North had been taken from their homes in the middle of the night and incarcerated in prisons, prison-ships, and, for the randomly chosen few, secret locations. They were all held without trial or charge. Those who had been brought to secret locations were tortured physically and psychologically. They were dressed in boiler suits, deprived of sleep, beaten, made to stand in overheated rooms on tiptoe until they collapsed hours later, revived and made to stand again, and throughout were subjected to a high-pitched 'white noise' which induced, in many, nervous breakdown. Now, one year later, many were still interned and would remain so for years to come. Hardly any of them were in the IRA.

Paddy Deery was. He had joined the youth wing of the IRA after internment was introduced. Though not allowed to carry arms, he had been trained in their use and promised induction as a fully fledged volunteer on his seventeenth birthday. On this day, as he watched the demonstration, he was sixteen.

*

A platoon of British soldiers also watched. Their presence in the area, on foot, was unusual. For the past twelve months, the army had been restricted to movement in armoured convoy. This was because the day after internment was introduced, the people had erected barricades at every conceivable entrance to the Bogside, Brandywell and Creggan, and proclaimed the 888-acre area 'Free Derry'. The barricades were powerful constructions, comprising metal girders cemented into the ground, with burnt-out vehicles piled on top. Five access roads, diligently monitored, were kept open to allow free movement of supplies, such as gas and foodstuffs, and limited public transport. The army occasionally roared down these roads in tanks, bringing supplies to their own troops, who were effectively locked into base in Free Derry. Attempted sorties on foot had led to gun-fights between the IRA and the army, with casualties on both sides, and occasionally vicious retribution, inflicted by the army on civilians. Kathleen Thompson, for instance, a mother of six, was shot dead, while standing in her garden in Creggan. Fifteen-year-old Manus Deery, a second cousin of Paddy, was shot dead while coming out of a fish-and-chip shop.

Nevertheless, the patrol now watching the demonstration was at confident ease, just as Paddy and the other spectators were. The reason for this was that a few days previously, on 31 July, the army had mounted a memorable assault on the area, codename Operation Motorman, of which Derry people still speak with awe.

The *Derry Journal* used front-page global terminology in order to convey to the people of a small town on an offshore island which had never been invaded in any of the World Wars or cold wars of the twentieth century, just what had happened to them:

Not since Russian troops entered Budapest and Prague in the 1950s and 1960s to suppress risings of the Czechoslovakian and Hungarian peoples have sights been seen in any European city like those in Derry yesterday morning. 1500 British soldiers followed 300 army vehicles in a massive invasion of the Bogside and Creggan estates.

The paper related how the commander of the British Land Forces had sealed off the main Derry-Donegal border roads and launched barges carrying fifty-ton Centurion tanks up the River Foyle to the Northern city 'invading Irish territorial waters' en route, in order to effect an assault by land on the people of Derry. With the town blocked off from the South, and blocked off by a sealed bridge from the rest of the North, the British Empire was attempting, said the Nationalist Party, 'a defence, which would eventually founder, of its last pathetic outpost, Derry. The British can shoot us, imprison us, starve us, but they will never defeat us.'

The Journal agreed. Though the army had again entered Bogside via Rossville Street, 'where the paratroopers had shot dead 13 Derry people only six months before', it would not prevail. The newspaper quoted the calm appraisal of Operation Motorman made by Mr John Hume MP, who represented Derry at Westminster: 'The British Army is not welcome. They will not be regarded as protectors of the people of Derry.'

Nevertheless, tanks which were bigger than Bogside houses had rolled over the barricades and Free Derry was taken with only two shots, which killed two unarmed teenage spectators, one of whom was later revealed to be a member of the IRA. The IRA had been stood down for the night.

This did not affect the IRA's standing in the community. Its refusal to engage the British Army in face-to-face confrontation was generally regarded as a wise move. Indeed, seven thousand teenagers had turned out, feet stamping in military fashion, for the funeral of the unarmed teenage volunteer, Seamus Bradley, who had merely been watching when the British Army crushed Free Derry. The funeral of the other youth was, by ominous contrast, a quiet, small, family affair.

Seamus Bradley's funeral was a harbinger of the future. Teenage members of the IRA's youth wing, such as Paddy Deery, moved as comfortably in the community as fish in water, and on this day, as he stood watching the anti-internment demonstration, he stood as a respectable young citizen of the town.

The soldiers who also watched the drama had exacted admission at gunpoint. Their status could not have been more different than it was only three years previously, in 1969, when they had replaced the police in Derry and been welcomed as saviours. Now they watched themselves being portrayed as imperialist invaders. This change was still a source of puzzlement to them. Despite internment, Bloody Sunday and Operation Motorman, they saw themselves as impartial.

They had been shot at and killed by both sides. They felt that they were keeping the warring factions apart. This painful confusion was poignantly expressed in a letter which an English soldier's father sent to the *Derry Journal* after Bloody Sunday. The letter was signed, complete with home address. In the current cold-war atmosphere, such a signed letter would be unthinkable but then, when war was still strange, the neighbouring islanders spoke to each other in mutual grief: 'Once we had an only son,' wrote Mr Frank Moon, of Clitheroe in Lancashire, England, to the people of Derry. 'He was a kindly man with a passion for ornithology and wild-life preservation, and a great sense of humour, and a basic belief in the rule of law.' This only son had just been killed by the IRA. Mr Clitheroe did not understand why but he wanted, hoped and expected that two island peoples divided by a stretch of water, would recognise each other's humanity. In talking thus to Irish people, about the ending of 'a young life of such infinite promise' this Englishman was paying a tribute and honour which is rare today, on either side.

*

At that time nevertheless, 1972, and on this day, 9 August, the Third Royal Regiment of Welsh Fusiliers stood with guns amidst a crowd of hostile unarmed Derry people. Catcalls were exchanged as the re-enactment of internment progressed. Three rubber bullets were fired by the soldiers. No one was hit. The patrol sergeant later said that they had seen a man carrying a gun, that a whistle had been blown to alert the crowd which then dispersed, and that the gunman had then fired one round. 'Typical IRA tactic to use the crowd for cover and I don't think the crowd realises this,' said the sergeant. He did not explain how a gunman could use a dispersed crowd for cover, nor why the army should fire at a crowd after a gunman had disappeared. The demonstration came to a halt while the people discussed the army fire. They were not afraid. They were outraged. Despite Bloody Sunday, they still believed that soldiers had no right to shoot at demonstrators. So they did what was common at that time. They sent for a local activist, whose *bona fides* were recognised by the army, and negotiations were entered into.

Paddy Deery stood in the crowd while Paddy Doherty spoke with the troops. After some conversation, Mr Doherty and the soldiers agreed to refer the matter to a higher authority. They would go to the nearest army camp and ask the commanding officer to judge whether or not the troops had had the right to fire rubber bullets at the crowd. Mr Doherty got into an army jeep, borrowed a loud-hailer from the soldiers, and spoke to the people. He was not under arrest, he assured them. In fact, it was his intention, once arrived in the camp, to have charges preferred against those soldiers who had fired the rubber bullets.

Off they went, leaving a six-man foot patrol of the Fusiliers alone in a crowd which was several hundred strong. Tempers were high. A demonstrator engaged the soldiers in dialogue. A stone was thrown while they talked. A soldier immediately fired another rubber bullet at head-height and close quarters into the crowd. The bullet left the muzzle of the gun at two hundred miles per hour. It was 4 inches long and $1\frac{1}{2}$ inches wide. 'A youth fell to the ground,' the *Derry Journal* recorded. The crowd retreated, returned, and more stones were thrown as the youth was dragged away by local people. More rubber bullets were fired, a Saladin tank arrived which disgorged extra troops, more talks were held, and a deal was worked out. The army would withdraw from the scene if guarantees were given that no more stones would be thrown. It was so agreed, and peace was restored, and both sides saved face.

The injured youth was brought to hospital, where a surgeon removed Paddy Deery's irreparably damaged left eye. His mother was just leaving home, to go over to hospital for a check-up on her own wounds, when the news was brought to her by her local priest, Fr George McLaughlin. When Paddy regained consciousness, Peggy was at his bedside, where she had waited through most of the night in the company of Fr Tom O'Gara. When he woke up, her son did not remember what had happened and he did not know how long he had been unconscious. He did not know that he had undergone an operation. Peggy told Paddy what had happened to him. The mother and the priest spent hours consoling the weeping boy. Fr O'Gara sang for Paddy. Among the songs he sang was 'The Patriot Game', the premier Irish anthem of the struggle for independence and freedom from the British:

Come all ye young rebels, and list while I sing,
For love of one's country is a terrible thing.
It banishes fear with the speed of a flame,
And makes us all part of the patriot game.
I was barely sixteen when I wandered away,
With a local battalion of the bould IRA ...

*

When Paddy got out of hospital in September, it was to find that the British Army had established a new camp behind the street in which he lived, breathing down his neck, hemming him in. Before he reached his seventeenth birthday that November, Paddy was on the run, in his own town, as a fully fledged member of the Provisional IRA. He slept in a different house every night. His expertise was as a driver of getaway cars. He had the fearlessness of youth, and the advantage over the soldiers of being welcome in his own town, despite the devastation then being wreaked, and the rising death toll.

Buildings were blown up on a near daily basis; one restaurant was blown up twice in one week. Attitudes to this state of affairs bordered on the cavalier, particularly among the people of no property for whom there was no prospect of ever owning property. Then, as now, in Derry, unemployment remained endemic above 20 per cent. In Catholic areas like Creggan, where Paddy lived, it was more than 50 per cent.

His IRA friend from those days recalls the cheek and swagger which characterised their actions. They hijacked a taxi once, drove into a factory, did not bother to disguise themselves with balaclavas, ordered the workers outside at gun-point, and planted a bomb. On their way back into Creggan, the taxi was stopped by a foot-patrol. An English soldier, newly arrived in Derry on a tour of duty, peered inside, and asked them their names, ages and addresses. Paddy slipped the gun he was holding under the seat, opened the door, jumped out and harangued the soldier about denying him his freedom in his own city. He challenged the soldier to guess his identity, mocking him, giving him a choice of the names of the six Deery brothers, oblivious to the fact that he had a distinctive identity mark, one glass eye. The soldier, a lost stranger, would not have known this about him.

By the standards of even those heady days, Paddy was headstrong and careless and he was expelled from the IRA for a time. The marriage which settled him at the age of twenty paradoxically prepared the way for a return to the ranks.

A Welfare War

Peggy and her
grandchildren
outside
82 Creggan
Heights

Regardless of what has happened since, the people of Derry
were in a worse condition before 1968. When Vincent
Kavanagh inherited his father's medical practice in the
nineteen-sixties, he found himself treating families in decay.
The illness which permeated the bodies and spirits of his
patients, old and young, was a reflection of the city in which
they lived. Derry was a political slum. His father told him
that the people he treated would survive poverty and
disease and overcrowding. Their real sickness, he said, was
apathy.

When the Civil Rights Movement began in 1968, the mental health of the people was enhanced. Despite the grief and suffering and hardening of heart which followed that initial blossoming, the real sickness has not returned. Vincent Kavanagh no longer feels despair.

Peggy Deery responded with alacrity to the change in mood. She was thirty-five years of age when she first marched down the hill from Creggan and made herself known to every agitator in town.

Those who knew her in the initial stage of revolt still recall with shock how poor she was. Carmel McCafferty, then a teenage apprentice-hairdresser, visited Peggy in the company of Bernadette Devlin, the newly elected Westminster MP for Mid-Ulster. 'We brought a bag of coal. Her electricity had been cut off and I had to go and get candles. There was a man lying sick in bed and the smell of his sickness filled the room. There were children everywhere. Me and my friend Marie washed and scrubbed and cleaned her house that night while she put the children to bed. Bernadette organised a collection to pay her electricity bill. People gave shillings from their dole money.'

When Peggy died in 1988, aged fifty-four, she was still in debt. Her electricity bill showed that she was in arrears to the tune of £972.89; the outstanding rent on her house amounted to £512.63. It is perfectly normal for Derry people living on welfare to die in such debt today. There is no shame in this. It is a small sign of victory in an extension of the war with Britain; the poor, lacking any other means, have opened up a welfare front from behind which they parry the legislation which Britain has deployed since 1968 in an effort to quell their revolt.

*

The economic war began in that year, 1968, when slum-dwelling Catholics started to squat in empty council houses. This action was in contravention of every moral standard by which they had been reared; respect for property and for law and order is ingrained in Catholic social teaching. It was a Derrywoman called Brigid Bond, slum-dweller extraordinaire, who reached for the higher moral ground, putting the rights of the family before those of property. She put her followers into vacant homes. The publicity which attended the confrontation between them and city sheriffs and legislators, intent on eviction, had a dramatic effect. Life infused statistics.

The statistics were numbing. The Catholic majority in Derry was ruled by the Protestant minority. This situation was brought about by the infamous gerrymander system. Local elections in 1967 resulted in 20,102 Catholic householders returning 8 nationalists, while 10,274 Protestant householders returned 12 Unionists.

Before Brigid Bond led the revolt, the Derry Corporation built 99 houses per year. Following abolition of the corporation in 1968, the Housing Executive built 840 houses a year.

Direct action does not pay the rent, however, nor does it feed and clothe people who have secured shelter. There were never any factories to squat into. The Catholic majority in Derry has won control of a town in which there are few jobs. Under Unionist rule, unemployment was static and sullen at 20 per cent. Since the British Government assumed direct rule of Northern Ireland in 1972, unemployment in Derry has climbed to 25 per cent, rising to 80 per cent in Catholic areas. Only one of Peggy Deery's fourteen children has ever held a steady permanent job.

*

Condemned as she was to a life-sentence at subsistence level, Peggy's financial ingenuity was challenged. When the Catholic political leadership in the North asked its people to withhold rent and rates from the government, Peggy did not look the gift-horse in the mouth. The rent-strike was deemed the only non-violent option available as a protest against internment in 1971. Peggy and her council-house peers responded at once, despite the risk of jail. Had they been liable for rates, they would have withheld them too. The leadership was confident of success. They were also disorganised. They were in no position to collect the monies withheld by one third of the population and lodge them in a bank. In any case, and in most cases, the weekly rent was converted into steak as the people dined in royal defiance of the enemy. A decision was swiftly taken that, come what may, there would be no retrospective payment of monies owed to the Unionist Government. This statement fell as music on Peggy's ears. The rent would never, ever, have to be repaid. It was expected that the authorities would buckle in face of such anarchy. They did not. The Unionist Government was abolished, the British instituted direct rule, and internment continued until 1975. Peggy withheld her rent during all those years. The British Government retaliated with the introduction of the Payment for Debt (Emergency Provisions) Act, Northern Ireland, 1971. As its title shows, the Act was not applied anywhere else in the United Kingdom. It became a weapon, used even after internment and the rent strike had ended, for clawing back from the welfare classes any and every penny, owed under any circumstances whatever, to the State.

The Act governed Peggy's income until the end of her days. She never knew from one week to the next, from 1971 until 1988, exactly how much money would be paid to her after deductions at source. An increase in widow's pension, reduction in rent, the rise and fall of tariffs on electricity, the shrinking value of her children's allowance, were all governed by the Act, which applied a sliding scale of punishment the dimensions of which were as readable as the entrails of a crow. In her handbag after her death, her children found a letter sent to Peggy by the Department of Health and Social Welfare. It read:

The Department of Finance and Personnel has, under the above Act, directed that the sum of £13.56 per week shall be taken out of your widow's pension towards reducing your electricity arrears from 13 April 1987 until the debt is discharged. As this is less than your present contribution of £13.87 the arrears will continue to increase.

*

As long as the electricity stayed on, Peggy did not worry unduly. The British Army were very keen that the houses which they raided should be well lit to facilitate their hunt for the IRA. With one arm of the bureaucracy pitted against another, there was always a chance for the poor.

The army also provided opportunities by reducing the street lighting in Derry, the better to protect soldiers on patrol. The streets, ravaged by war, are the occasion of many accidents and claims for compensation. Peggy success-fully sued the Department of the Environment on two occasions.

Derry has become known as 'pothole city', an appellation as cynical as it is accurate. It is widely accepted that not all who claim damages have sustained injury from falling into potholes. It is difficult for the British Government to refute the claims, since police do not patrol the streets, the army is in too much of a hurry to notice, property is regularly damaged by the security forces in smash-and-grab raids for weapons, and barricades spring up regularly. Also, the people of Derry have learned to show as much disregard for the awesome obligations of truth under British oath as have the guardians of law and order. The testimony of the Bloody Sunday regiment, which was not rejected by the Court of Inquiry, set the standard. Commenting on the outcome of the inquiry, the leader of the Nationalist Party, Eddie McAteer, said, 'At least the judge didn't find the dead guilty of committing suicide.'

The corrosion of morality is captured in an apocryphal story about pothole city. One man says to another man on crutches, 'Have you been to see your solicitor?' The cripple replies: 'I saw him before I fell.'

There was no government challenge to Peggy's claim of falling. The injuries sustained on Bloody Sunday had left her with a shortened leg and a foot without feeling. The shortest journey resulted in chafed and bleeding skin around a hole in her heel that never healed. She fell con-stantly. The British Army called her 'chicken-leg'.

Soldiers cheerfully signed chits for damages to her home after each ransack. The Emergency Provisions Act, also exclusive to the North, allows them to wreck doors, windows, floorboards and furniture at will. Refurbishment by government is slow, the tardiness excused on grounds of cost and cut-backs in public expenditure, and the increasing expense of maintaining a standing army in the North.

*

The British Army was the direct cause of Peggy Deery's acquisition of what was, in welfare terms, a fortune. The government paid her £14,000 compensation for her Bloody Sunday injuries. She lavished a great portion of that on her son Paddy. Money was also spent on family travel to the various prisons where some of her children were lodged as they reaped the bitter harvest of involvement after Bloody Sunday; each prison visit also meant the expense of a food parcel, and money lodged for cigarettes for the prisoner. Peggy supported also out of her fortune those of her children who fled across the border, seeking refuge or escape.

It did not last, but while it lasted she was generous, distributing cash gifts on the birthdays of her children and grandchildren and of her sisters and brothers, and at Christmas. As the fortune dwindled, she was obliged to cut the sums in half. A seasonal note to her sister Nellie caught her mood exactly as she faced a return to poverty:

Dear Nellie,
Here is a fiver. I'm sorry Nellie, it's all I can give you. Between children and grandchildren I'm effed off.
Love,
Peggy.

*

She never relinquished the most obvious status of wealth. The telephone which was at first an indulgence became a necessity as Peggy Deery kept urgent track of her fourteen children's whereabouts. The calls at dawn came invariably from police stations or hospitals or priests or solicitors. She learned because of the phone that one of the most enduring myths about the wartime North was untrue. This was that people who ran up telephone bills would never be cut off if they had an IRA relative in the family. Despite Paddy's involvement, and army interest in him, Peggy's phone was cut off in 1986 when he spent a short period in jail.

The family had a collection and the bill was paid. The government-run company accepted the money and sent her a letter which left her furious:

> You are required to pay a further amount of £150 by way of security for payment in respect of further service. Deposit will be retained for a minimum of one year. The rate of interest is 6 per cent per annum.

Peggy wrote this off as a bad investment and had a new line installed in the married name of one of her daughters. The government's computer intelligence was unable to cope with such a ruse. The cost of the new installation was minimal, and of course the new client had a credit-worthy reputation which would ensure years of debt-in-good-faith.

*

In the last twelve months of her life, Peggy Deery's welfare war was fought by a woman so ill that the government agreed in 1987 to pay an attendance allowance for one of the daughters who lived with her. Though she was then bed-ridden the allowance was calculated on the basis of an eight-hour day. The melonin dressings for her permanently wounded foot, the plastic gloves which her daughters used when cleaning out its foul skin tissue, the pills for blood pressure, the pills for sleeping, and the anti-depressant pills were provided free by the Health Service. On the other hand she lost her child-benefit allowance for the last of her children, Bernadette, who was adjudged adult and ready for work. Peggy wept on the day Bernadette's national insurance number came through the post. Her income was further reduced; her sixteen-year-old daughter, number NX575664D, raised in war, faced a future of war; Peggy's thirty-two years of non-stop mothering were officially over in 1987.

The government letter which formally ended her responsibility for the last-born of her children came in September. Peggy Deery died of cardiac arrest four months later.

I Love You, Mammy

Margie, Kevin and
their children

Since she became an auxiliary nurse in Altnagelvin Hospital,
Peggy's eldest daughter Margie has acquired an understanding of sickness that she did not have when her father
was bed-ridden with cancer. She is familiar with, and now
sympathetic to, the rage to which very sick people are
driven, often against their will and their better nature. This
has enabled her to look back with charity and gentleness to
the life they all had to endure while their father suffered
helplessly. 'A disc was removed from his back and he wore a
plastic jacket to his spine. It cut into the bottom of his back.
He had an open wound. You could see right into it. There
was a growth there like a cauliflower.'

Margie helped her mother change the dressings that covered the seeping hole in her father's back. There was a smell off it. It seeped through her childhood. She was fourteen when her father died after years of agony. 'He wanted painkillers all the time, and he wouldn't go into hospital, and the doctor wouldn't increase the dosage. He just gave us blank prescriptions for more and more dressings and bandages. My mother filled in her own prescription, for Diaconal, forged the doctor's signature, and I'd go to a different chemist every day.' Her father's bed was moved into the living room, so that they could give him constant attention while also looking after the babies. Peggy relied heavily on the girl to help her run the home.

On Christmas Eve, 1970, the last Christmas of her father's life, his temper boiled to the point where the family had to evacuate the house. 'If you came within reach of him, he'd have killed you.' Peggy, pregnant for the last time, walked the streets that night with her thirteen children. That was the worst night, looking in at other people's houses, and the Christmas decorations and wishing they had somewhere to sleep. 'It was a question of waiting until you knew he'd gone to sleep himself.'

The little caravan, pushing prams, clutching infants by the hand, had had to walk the streets before. Sometimes they went to stay with uncles and aunts. 'Can you picture it, a clatter of children and my ma, landing in unexpectedly looking for a bed? Sure nobody would ever have enough beds. We spent one night with our heads resting in our arms over somebody's table. It was always wild embarrassing in the morning, with us and them trying to go to the one toilet, make breakfast, wash ourselves, and then what do you do? Keep sitting around while one of us went to check if it was alright to go home?'

On nights when they felt they'd exhausted their welcome with relatives, they'd land in on some neighbour. 'For a visit, and a cup of tea. Me ma, and however many there were of us. Nine, ten, eleven, it grew every year. We'd leave the neighbour around midnight, as though it was the most normal thing in the world. It was rotten. I will never forget that.'

More often than not, they'd stay at home and suffer their father's wrath. It was less humiliating. Peggy took many blows. Margie often hid in the coalshed or the dog kennel. 'The hospital job was a blessing. I can understand now. I can remember the good times too, more than the others, because I was around him long enough, and was old enough, to know. The others were too small. Like, when he was well, in the early days, we'd wake up in the morning and he'd have all our shoes polished and lined up in front of the fire. The fire was always lit by the time we got up. There'd be a big plate of toast, and a bowl of boiled eggs, and the shoes shining like glass. My father was very neat. He'd clean the house like a whirlwind.'

Every summer he rented a house across the border in parts of Donegal that had not then become fashionable. The cost was minimal, because living in isolated areas was equated with the peasant condition and most Derry people preferred day-trips by bus to a crowded resort where they could buy ice-cream and chips and shelter in cafés when it rained. 'Right enough, we were like a gypsy family, running around in the wilds. The houses where he'd park us had dry toilets. They were on the beach or the hill, and you'd run straight into the water. There was more room in the Atlantic than there was in the house.' Today, the holiday homes in Inch island, Lisfannon and Cockhill command a fortune in rent.

Her father cooked meals in the open, on driftwood they gathered. He'd stand on the beach, in sunset, teasing his hungry brood and singing 'Nobody's Child'.

Wherever he went he brought his two redsetters, Rusty and Bingo, kingly animals, reared in a town that was used to mongrels and greyhounds. At least the greyhounds might win the odd race and earn a few shillings. Margie remembers the flowers he planted and the hedge he tended in the garden around the wretched tinny bungalow which passed for suitable housing for the Catholic working-class, in Creggan.

Then came the illness, and the rage against the world,

against his own family, against his own wife and little children, no matter how much they tried to take care of him and soothe him. Before he became totally bed-ridden, his weight reduced to eighty-four pounds of skin and bones and raw flesh, his sisters in America invited him over for a holiday. 'The day he left for America, we all cheered. We jumped up and down in the living-room, me mammy and all of us, with our arms round each other, skipping and jumping. We were going to have peace for six weeks. Me ma wouldn't be thumped.' He returned home unexpectedly after three weeks. 'When we heard he was coming back home, it was like we'd been given news of a disaster. Total depression. And fear. Me da was like Jekyll and Hyde, you see.'

Peggy used to veer between fury and sentiment when she and Margie would look at his memoriam card, and talk about him, after his death in October 1971.

*

Margie was on her second date with her future husband Kevin, in January 1972, when she heard her mother had been shot. She and Kevin had been to a young people's dance, run in the parish hall in Creggan. It was known as the Diddler's Disco. They were in the grounds of the chapel, courting, when she was told. She never returned to school.

It was six weeks before the children were allowed to see their mother. Fr O'Gara helped ferry them to Belfast to where she had been transferred. They had to put on sterilised white boots, aprons and hats. Their mother did not know them. Even in their ordinary clothes, she would not have recognized them. Feverish, jittery and hallucinating, her skin a jaundiced yellow, she was interested only in her fizzy lemonade. She thought the doctor had stolen her fizzy lemonade. The children thought their mother had lost her mind.

She had certainly lost her confidence. When Peggy was returned to hospital in Derry, Margie asked her why she concealed a newspaper photograph of her children under her pillow. It had been printed after Bloody Sunday. Peggy said she didn't want to upset anyone passing through the ward; that you'd never know who might be snooping around looking to shoot someone.

A social worker came to see the children while Peggy was in hospital. She thought that the old paraffin heater, fuming and spluttering in the corner, which Margie had lit against the wintry cold, was dangerous. Margie would not let the woman turn the heater off. Nor would she entertain the suggestion that the children should be put in an orphanage. Nine of the Deerys were eight years of age and under. They included two sets of twins and the baby. Margie, who had just turned fifteen, said the family would remain together in the house. She and Paddy would look after Helen, Johnny, Owney, Pio, Michael, the twins May and Bridie, twins Bess and Tony, Martin, June and the infant Bernadette.

Peggy came home from hospital that summer in a wheel-chair, a caliper strapped to her leg. She could barely manage to move on crutches. Margie hoped her mother would like the different and better council house into which an uncle had squatted them in her absence. It was made of brick and had four bedrooms. Fr O'Gara helped the young squatters redecorate for Peggy's homecoming. He and Margie chose the paint and wallpaper. The older children wielded brush and paste, the younger children played with the baby, and they all lined up at the front door, the priest and these children, to welcome Peggy out of the ambulance which brought her to her new home. The pleasure was short-lived. Peggy was scarcely out of hospital than she had to go back daily to visit Paddy.

*

Peggy taught Margie to wheel and deal with the skill of a stockbroker against the expected government compensation for Peggy's injuries. A Bloody Sunday fund for victims had also been set up to adminster the contributions that poured in from around the world. 'I had a track worn down to P.K. O'Doherty's house,' says Margie. Her mother sent her constantly to the home of the fund administrator, seeking subs to supplement her widow's pension. There was some flamboyance – hardly was the house furnished courtesy of contributions than Peggy decided to move again. A house right beside her sister Nellie had become vacant, the family squatted in, and they lived side by side in numbers 80 and 82 Creggan Heights, sharing responsibility for the merged tribes. Peggy gave away those pieces of recently bought furniture which did not fit the new dimensions, renovated once more, and settled down. This was to be her last and final home.

It backed onto the new camp which the British Army had erected, as it dug in for a long stay in the city. Creggan Heights was the very last row of houses in the estate. Behind it, across a few fields, lay the border, and the Republic of Ireland. The soldiers pitched camp on Piggery Ridge, interposing themselves between the street and the border. The camp straddled the road, facing down into Creggan, facing down its people, who were now physically ghettoised. The soldiers were literally within a stone's throw of the Deery children, of all the children in the street, and the children frequently stood in their back gardens, throwing stones at the soldiers.

Peggy borrowed lavishly against her promised compensation of £14,000 in an attempt to buy freedom for her children. The toys and gifts did not seduce them away from the battlefield which was now their playground.

She concentrated a lot on feeding her children. Sunday dinner was a spectacular event, for which they would religiously gather. On weekdays they would dribble in and out at odd hours, but on Sundays they were expected to be all present and correct at the appointed time. They were more than that – they were delighted to gather round their mother on that day, as she told and re-told her ambition, that she might keep them all with her, in one big house, all their lives, all of them and their own children too, safe and sound around her. She was a great cook, says Margie. 'There'd be turkey and ham and gravy and sprouts and carrots and ice-cream and jelly, even if it wasn't Christmas.'

One Christmas she remembers in particular from that time. The compensation had not yet come through, but her mother sent her up to the bank to borrow against it. It was not Margie's first visit there. 'Ma knew she was pushing her luck a wee bit, again, but she bought two boxes of cigars and told me to have a go. In I went. The bank manager said he was off cigars.'

*

Margie got married on 19 February 1977, at the age of twenty. Kevin was twenty-three. The couple represented on their wedding day a young generation the like of which Derry may not see again for a long time. They had known a childhood without war, with a stable social structure, complete with rules and taboos and agreed morality; they went as virgins to the altar.

The £14,000 had by then come through, and been gone through, and Peggy blew what was left on their wedding. The reception was held at Keaveney's Hotel in Moville, across the border. The hotel was the height of social respectability. It did not matter any more that a passing foot patrol had pretended that morning to vomit as Margie emerged from Creggan Heights in her finery. The wedding breakfast had been so delicious, and the eighty guests so happy, and the day so promising in its splendour, that Peggy insisted they all stay on for afternoon tea, which she paid for.

The fortune was now gone.

Margie and Kevin moved into a flat in the heart of town, in Shipquay Street. She visited her mother daily. Kevin and she often spent their evenings in Creggan Heights, consoling her mother, as the family became decimated by the war. The house was constantly raided, the boys were going in and out of jail or on the run, the younger girls too had started to enter the prison system, for non-attendance at school.

One night, as they were walking down Shipquay Street to their flat, Margie burst into tears. Why, Kevin asked. 'We're going home to a press full of messages [groceries] and my mother has nothing in hers.' Peggy had taught her children that a kitchen with a fully stocked press was the unshakeable foundation of a happy family. Kevin returned immediately by taxi to Creggan Heights, stopping off to buy messages. He brought Peggy sausages and eggs and tinned food for her kitchen press, and a bag of coal for her hearth.

Kevin, Margie and Peggy then entered into a complex financial relationship. Kevin would advance Peggy sixty pounds on a Friday to see her through the weekend, particularly the ever-expanding Sunday dinner. To the fourteen children were now added Kevin, and Paddy's wife, and the growing number of grandchildren. On Tuesday, Peggy cashed her widow's pension and family allowance. On Thursday she got what the unemployed teenagers collected from the dole. On Friday morning she redistributed the cash, giving pocket-money to her sons and daughters, and sending Kevin the sixty pounds she owed him. On Friday night, he brought it back again.

Margie delighted in giving her mother pocket-money from her own wages. In 1981, at the age of twenty-four, she had taken up her first-ever paid job as an auxiliary nurse to help pay the mortgage of the new house which she and Kevin had just bought. It was the first and only private home ever acquired by any of the Deery children. This was a landmark in the family history and Peggy exulted in it.

Margie combines her nursing career with rearing children, of which she now has four, including a set of twins. The family has been planned, an increasingly accepted feature of Derry life. Though she works from eight at night until eight in the morning, three and a half days a week, the child-rearing difficulties have been easily circumvented. Kevin was recently made redundant from his clerical job with a building firm and her brothers and sisters are frequent visitors to her house.

Margie consciously spoils her children, taking particular pleasure with her first-born, Leanne, on whom she showered a profusion of toys and clothes. Peggy remarked on this once: 'You're getting Leanne far too much.' Margie explained, 'I'm getting her the things I never had.' Peggy burst into tears. She had done her best; she would have given young Margie such things if she could; it had not been possible. Margie thought about this for days, and then

approached her mother. Of course Leanne was getting far
too much. 'I'm not buying them for her, Ma. I'm buying her
things I really wanted for myself. I'm pretending to be your
wain all over again, only this time it's even better.' She
recalled for Peggy the number of times Peggy had sat in
proud poverty, delighted with her brood, saying, 'You could
have worse than wains.' Peggy had always made them feel
important, a bonus in her life, not a drag. Peggy had made
them feel like fourteen gifts.

'I'm glad I came right out and spoke to her that day. It's a
wild embarrassing thing to talk like that to your mother. It's
very hard to look her right in the eye and say "I love you",
and I never said it in so many words, unless you count cards
on Mother's Day and things like that. If there were medals
for mothers, my mother would get every one of them. I told
her that.'

*

Margie recounts, in so many words, her love for Kevin. 'He
used to go missing on me. I didn't mind. I knew where he
was. He was up playing Scrabble with Peggy, or "I spy" or
two-hand patience. I was able to go to bed in peace. I knew
she wasn't alone, sitting there by herself, worrying about
everybody.'

Kevin had experienced at first-hand the worry of another
woman sitting alone, not knowing if her child was dead or
alive. One night his friend's wife had phoned him. Her
daughter had gone missing. Her husband was in London,
where he had gone to watch Barry McGuigan capture the
world featherweight boxing championship. While Ireland,
North and South, celebrated that famous victory, Kevin sat
with the woman in a home where horror reigned.

The IRA went round the homes and haunts of known
gangsters, kicking in doors, threatening retribution if the
girl was harmed. She returned home safely next day.

Whenever he sits down in his own home, Kevin
invariably gathers his twins into his arms, holding them
against harm, holding them easily even as he sleeps in the
armchair. He always drives visitors home if it is late, par-

ticularly young people. Kevin has become adept now at handling and soothing the complications of family life, particularly at the great ritual moments. It was he who dissuaded Paddy from pulling an unwelcome relative off the bus chartered to bring guests to the wedding of himself and Margie.

The protection of home and family life is precious to him.

In her own home, with Kevin or others, Peggy was afforded some protection, particularly from insult. 'She would ask me to go the rounds of the police stations for her, looking for whichever one had been hauled in,' says Margie. 'One night she sent me down a pressure cooker, with Paddy's dinner in it. I brought it along to the Strand Road station, and the policeman said there was enough in it to feed Paddy and all the cops. Even Paddy couldn't miss seeing that, with his one eye, he said. That's the mentality you have to deal with. How's chicken-leg, they'd say about me ma.

'There's this one policeman my mother dreaded meeting. One night he stopped the taxi I was in. "I'm surprised to see you having sluts in your car," he said to the driver. The taxi-driver said he was only doing his job; he didn't defend me. When my mother used to see this policeman she'd pretend to laugh. Then she would go home and cry.'

Cagney and Lacey

Sandra and Peggy

It was Fr O'Gara who persuaded Peggy that a mother did not have to stay fulltime at home, and that a widow should enjoy herself without fear of attracting social odium. She was forty-five years of age when he arranged her second debut, in 1978, into the outside world of men and women, of dancing, dining, and drinking. Though Margie was married and away, Helen and Pio were now young women and able to help run the home.

The transition was not easily accomplished. Besides an understandable apprehension, Peggy felt deeply embarrassed about being physically crippled. The priest enlisted the help of Peggy's niece and god-child Sandra, then aged twenty-two. She was in the second year of her marriage. The marriage had settled her husband who became what Sandra called 'a real house-man. He loved staying at home. He wouldn't go out and dance. My mother and my granny were out dancing together. So I was glad when Fr O'Gara told me to go out dancing with Peggy.'

He pointed out the advantages of this arrangement. Each woman could protect the other's reputation; each woman, he teased Sandra, could take the bare look off the other.

The duo quickly dubbed themselves Cagney and Lacey, after their soap-opera heroines of the time. Peggy with her prematurely whitened hair and Sandra with her dark mane embarked on a series of social adventures of which, they were sure, the New York cops Cagney and Lacey would have been proud. 'One night we hadn't the taxi-fare across the border, and it was snowing, but we walked all the way from Creggan to a pub in Bridgend, eating toffee apples.' The five-mile hike did not make Peggy's deadened foot bleed any more than a walk to Sunday mass at her local chapel.

They had begun their social career with rather more caution, going first to bingo in the Creggan parish hall with Peggy's mother. Then they attended a weekly old-timers' dance, in the same hall, in the company of Peggy's sister Nellie, Sandra's mother. The foursome was completed by Peggy McLaughlin, a neighbour who was chairwoman of the tenants' association and a member of Sinn Féin. The combined credentials of these women were the height of respectability. Lustre was added to their reputation by Nellie's standing in Derry as a ballroom-dancing champion. People would clear the floor to watch her do the tango. She could lead as easily as she could follow, and she led the other three with nonchalance into society.

All the same, her younger sister and even younger daughter preferred a faster tempo. Their peer groups congregated in pubs and inns across the border and as their confidence increased, their social circle widened. Sandra had a natural empathy with Peggy's reticence about her disability. 'When I was seventeen, I got a gum disease and all my teeth were taken out. I was affronted and wouldn't leave the house. Peggy came down and told me to try on me da's false teeth. When my own were fitted she made me to go to a dance in St Mary's Community Centre. I got one dance all night, from a boy who was a simpleton. I remember I wore a long purple frock.'

Peggy wore nothing but trousers since she was shot. Sandra used to 'feel guilty about wearing skirts'. One of Peggy's legs was now shorter than the other, and the calf on her damaged leg was noticeably thinner. This was not so obvious when she wore knee-high boots, and Sandra gradually coaxed her into frocks and boots in winter. Peggy's old flair for fashion returned, and her legendary ability to improvise. A lace nightdress, presented by one of her children, which she did not wish to waste in bed, was turned into a blouse. It was fastened at the waist with Paddy's dress-uniform IRA belt, converted for the occasion with white shoe-dye.

'One night I even got the two of us decked out in black sleeveless dresses. We went to a dance in Ballybofey. She wouldn't leave the ladies room. She said we looked like them singing sisters, The Campbells, that refused to retire. I said to her "We're lovely", and I got her to stroke my hair with a brush one hundred times, just like she used to when I was a child, then I brushed her hair one hundred times and then we hit the dance-floor. She was self-conscious, all the same. Wherever we went, she always made me walk in front of her, so nobody would notice her gimp.'

They worked out an identity and a routine for talking with men, and establishing social boundaries. They pretended they were inseparable sisters. They invented careers for themselves as nurses, a guaranteed conversation opener with those who would be unable to sustain chitchat about home, family and children. 'Some man would always say, "I've seen you before." Peggy would always say, "That was in the labour ward at Altnagelvin. I'm a midwife and I delivered your wife of your baby."'

They operated always together, on the basis of safety in numbers, and would sometimes be joined by one of Peggy's daughters. One night Peggy and Sandra and Pio found themselves after closing time on the Donegal side of the border without the price of a taxi home between them. They were offered a lift in a car containing three young men. The car stopped near Derry, at a sports complex, and the young men switched on the radio and asked them to waltz on the football pitch. Peggy's partner was well below average height. The little man and the limping woman enjoyed each other's disability.

Peggy usually checked the combined finances of Sandra and herself before going out for the evening, setting the taxi-fare home firmly aside in a special pocket of her purse. 'That's our guarantee of safe passage,' she would say. If money was scarce, they would have a few drinks before leaving the house. Neither woman had tasted alcohol before their Cagney and Lacey career began. Peggy liked Southern Comfort and white lemonade. Sandra liked Smirnoff vodka with ice cubes. Peggy sometimes managed to save on mixers by bringing her own bottle of white lemonade to the pubs.

She also established a method of getting a free round of drinks from management or admirers by the simple expedient of shoving Sandra on-stage in the singing pubs which they liked to frequent. Sandra had an excellent voice, and Peggy had an excellent memory for lyrics, so their country-and-western contributions were always welcome, with Peggy mouthing the words from her by now well-stocked table. 'She was strict about drinking, though. The minute I said I couldn't feel my nose, Peggy would say we'd had enough. It was a sure-fire system because every time I couldn't feel my nose I'd blurt right out and say so.'

*

The women discovered another form of entertainment when Peggy came under hypnosis on one of their nights out. 'We saw a billboard about the man who does Elvis impressions so we set off from Derry one night to see him.

We got the date wrong and when we arrived it was a man who hypnotises people. He asked for people to come up on the stage and Peggy volunteered. He put her in a trance and told her the man sitting beside her was Tom Jones. Peggy started fixing her hair and making eyes at this fellow, and then they produced a kitchen mop and made her dance with it, telling her this was Elvis Presley. Then she believed she was in Spain, and the heat was awful and she was being attacked by mosquitoes, and she started to take off her blouse. The man only let her undo the top button.'

Inspired, the women gave house parties, inviting a local entertainer to come along and hypnotise their guests. The guests were invited to contribute two pounds each towards his sixty-pounds fee. Given the size of the Deery clan, with cousins and aunts and friends and neighbours, and Peggy's induced imitation of Dolly Parton singing 'Jolene', there was often enough money left over with which to buy Southern Comfort and vodka.

The Cagney-and-Lacey team were once involved in a time-honoured highly personal interpretation of the import-export laws governing cross-border transactions. The price of booze and cigarettes in the North was the envy of the South. Peggy and Sandra fell in with a man who regularly filled his car with those items, bought at Northern prices, and regularly worried about the attentions of customs officials in the Republic. He persuaded the women that their company in his car, at such times, would distract the officials. They would be charmed by his efforts to bring his two passengers on a much needed jaunt from the war-torn North to the carefree South. The joy of the women as the car brought them over the border, heading towards pastures new in Sligo and Cork, was indeed as charming as it was distracting. Bemused Irish customs men neglected to search the vehicle as the women got out at border posts, and danced and sang and warbled the praises of the Free State into which they were escaping. They made too vivid an impression. No woman with a home and family to care for could possibly have so much free time. The customs officials began to take a closer interest. The Cagney-and-Lacey expeditions into the deep South came to an end.

*

Then Peggy acquired a suitor. He was a middle-aged bachelor who lived with his mother on a small farm in the North. He motored faithfully into Derry every week, and every week he found Peggy and Sandra dressed up and waiting for him in Peggy's kitchen. He wined and dined them, escorted them to the singing pubs and cabarets, drove them to bingo sessions in football fields where they had to blow whistles and pomp the horn if they won, and he deposited them both in Peggy's house when the evening should end.

The threesome found the arrangement comfortable. The shy bachelor had female company, and was never in a position where his virility would be challenged. The two women were pleased with the permanent escort of, as Sandra described him, 'a gentleman.' The car belonging to Peggy's suitor was very useful as the war started to split the family in a serious way, and some of Peggy's children went into seemingly permanent exile across the border. The transport meant that she could spend more evenings there with them. At one period in the eighties, Paddy, Helen, Johnny and Pio were living in scattered locations in Donegal. Peggy used to joke with her daughters about the new man in her life. 'I'll marry him if one of yous will sleep with him.'

Kicked to Death

Necky and his fiancée

Cagney and Lacey ended their careers when Peggy's son Michael was kicked to death in a disco brawl in Derry in 1986. He was the first of Peggy's children to die. Born in 1962 and buried just before his twenty-fourth birthday, he had known no life other than a life lived in a town at war. He was killed by members of his own community; by young men of his own age, from his own housing estate in Creggan. 'Is there life before death?' is the question posed by the most famous and poignant graffiti in Northern Ireland. The war has diminished the quality of life in Derry, just as civil revolt has enhanced it. There was no social outcry when Michael died: his life and death were accepted as fairly normal for a young man of his time.

His schoolgoing years, from 1968, when the Civil Rights Movement began, until he went, half-literate, aged seventeen, into a world of unemployment, were unexceptional. An offer had been made during his childhood to show him life without war, in England, on a free holiday for deprived children. A deprived child in Derry is any child who grew up or is growing up during the war in the North of Ireland. These free holidays are on offer all the time. Peggy wouldn't let her twelve-year-old son go on his holiday because he was still bed-wetting at that age. She didn't want him exposed to embarrassment. He was already suffering enough from a minor speech impediment. His inability to get his tongue round his own name as a child led to his nickname Necky. The impediment was due to stress, the doctor said, as was the bed-wetting.

Stress was unavoidable. The seventies were very bad years for any child trying to go to school. Army camps were pitched right beside school grounds then, and there was daily warfare between the army and the IRA. Since houses were nightly raided by the army, home was also a place of danger for the child, especially for one like Michael with a brother in the IRA.

Attempts were nevertheless made to make education appear normal. While Michael and his contemporaries braved their way through bullet and bomb, the Ministry for Education came up with a fairly typical scheme. A headmistress in Michael's area was given twenty-four hours' notice, by phone-call, from the Ministry, that a VIP was coming to pay a visit. The headmistress was ordered not to speak to anyone, not even the school board about the visit, for security reasons.

The visitor was Margaret Atkins, wife of the then secretary of state for Northern Ireland, Humphrey Atkins. She came, in secrecy, and whirled through the classrooms, while her armed Special-Branch escort patrolled the corridors. Tea and photographs were taken. It was intended to publish these photographs as proof of peace in Derry, and of the harmonious relationship between Northern Irish Catholics and their British rulers.

The children went home and told their parents about the visit. That night the school building and windows were daubed with slogans which declared that the headmistress was a 'cop-lover', and 'the future governor of Armagh Jail', the women's prison.

Next day, the head girl of the school arrived in a panic. She did not want any photograph of herself in the company of the VIP to be published in the press. She feared that her community would regard her as a traitor. That afternoon, a picket was placed on the school gates. The picketers were parents whose sons and daughters had been jailed or killed during Mr Humphrey Atkins' tenure as secretary of state for Northern Ireland. The parents were joined by pupils.

The head of the school board, Fr George McLaughlin, who had been inside discussing the situation with the head-mistress, drove his car towards the picket-line, got out, and chatted with the protesters. Then he drove away. The staff formed a convoy of cars and drove towards the picketers. The headmistress got out and engaged them in talk. They told her they did not wish to harm her, that she need not be frightened, but that they objected bitterly to the reception accorded the wife of their oppressor. They were humiliated at the thought that their children had been forced to sing for the VIP, and make sandwiches for her during cookery class.

The headmistress went on sick leave, and shortly after-wards took early retirement. The photographs were never published. The heads of all the schools in the area informed the Ministry of Education of their opinion that the head-mistress and her pupils had been hijacked; that the school had been effectively blackmailed by a government which could withdraw or cut back on educational funding; and that the children's lives had been put in danger by the presence of armed policemen, the avowed enemy of the IRA.

The Northern Ireland Office issued a statement regretting that an expression of genuine interest in the welfare of children had been turned into a political occasion.

That was the kind of atmosphere in which Michael Deery was educated.

*

He finished his schooling in jail, convicted of throwing petrol bombs at a police car. He had thrown them in Easter 1981, a year of desperation and tension in the North. Bobby Sands MP, Officer in Command of the IRA prisoners, was on hunger-strike in jail, and dying. An Easter parade in support of him had ended with the death, in Derry, of two teenagers, who had been run over by army jeeps. Michael joined in the subsequent riot, which went on until the small hours of the morning. His statement to police about the riot shows that at first the eighteen-year-old youth refused to answer their questions:

Answer: I don't like anyone that's loose in the mouth.
            I don't like people that tell anything they
            shouldn't. I wouldn't tell anyone anything.
Question: Isn't it true to say, Michael, that you support the
            IRA?
A: No.
Q: Isn't it true to say that you hate policemen?
A: Yes.
Q: Why's that?
A: Nothing.
Q: Why?
A: They stop me all the time.
Q: How many times have you been stopped?
A: I lost count.
Q: Did anything happen to you?
A: Nothing.
Q: So why should this annoy you?
A: I don't like getting stopped, just.

Then Michael made his statement. 'It was a Sunday night, me and X were walking around the Creggan. We walk around it every night just to see what's happening. Also, I can't sleep if I go to bed early. It was around two a.m. . .'

Convicted in the autumn, he received an eighteen-month sentence in a detention centre for young offenders. His sisters remember that he had his teeth fixed while in detention, and they teased him about being now the best looking of the Deery boys, which he was. He was taller than the rest of the family, and well built in contrast to their slight stature. He told them that he was going to class while in jail, and hoped to be able to read and write by the time he got out.

Towards the end of his sentence, he wrote a letter to Peggy, dated 23 November 1982. She kept it as a proud memento of his studies:

Well, mum,

I hope you and the family is doing alright. Tell Bridie I am glad she is getting engaged on her birthday and tell her I am sorry I won't be able to send her a present but I will send her a birthday card. Well mum, I hope everything is working out at the house for you and everything is allright. I was up in court on Monday for rioting last year, I got six months to run in with my other sentence. I am going to find a job next, if I can stay out of trouble. Well mum, I will be sending you all Xmas cards next week and I hope you're all having a terrific Christmas this year. It will be even happier next year because I will be with you all again. Well mum, here the days are flying in here. So it won't be long till I am out alltogether. I am still going to school in here because I want to learn to write and read better. Well mum, I can't think of anything to say so on tell I hear from you God bless yous all.

From Michael.

P.S. Write soon.

There was no job for him when he got out. Michael joined the dole. An application to join the adult wing of the IRA was turned down. He spent a lot of time child-minding for his oldest sister Margie and her husband Kevin, running their home and family for them by day. This entailed rising at dawn and walking several miles to their home in Pennyburn.

He was popular in his family. When his sisters appeared in the kitchen, dressed for a dance, they never knew which one he would scoop up into his arms, carry upstairs, and dump into the bath which he then filled with water. He spent a lot of time visiting Paddy, Helen and Pio who were across the border. In the beautiful mountain village in Donegal where Helen and her husband lived, he met and courted and arranged to marry a young local woman.

*

Two weeks before his wedding, he was involved in a brawl in the New York-New York nightclub in Derry. It ended when Michael was sent tumbling down a concrete staircase.

He spent the night in Altnagelvin Hospital and was transferred next morning to Belfast, where he was connected to a life-support machine. During that week there, those of his family who were not wanted by the police made the 180-mile round journey every day to see him. They hugged and kissed him and Margie promised God that not one of the Deerys would ever miss Sunday mass again. Necky's fiancée placed his hand on her stomach hoping he could feel his child high within and near birth. Peggy spoke to him constantly. 'Come on, Necky, don't do this to me.' The doctors switched off the machine at ten minutes to five one afternoon. Disbelieving, unwilling to look any more, his family went and waited next door. Tony and his wife Lily, and Margie's husband Kevin, kept final vigil with a priest. An hour later, Kevin went to see the others. He kissed Margie on the cheek. He confirmed the look on her face. 'Aye, he's dead.' While Peggy went to sit with her dead son, Margie made her brothers and sisters 'face the wall. Two this way, two that, and I told them to take a couple of kicks at the wall'. While their grief and anger burst she talked to them. She concentrated a lot on Johnny, who had been in the nightclub with Necky. She told him that had Necky lived, with his brain damaged and his body crippled, he would eventually have become only a hindrance. She spoke with the authority and love of a woman who had seen illness damage her father's capacity for love, who had seen family visits to the long-term ill in hospital gradually taper off in despair and guilt and sheer inability to cope.

She was speaking to young men who might go seeking revenge; to young women who might encourage it. The kicks she had given the wall herself were sufficient warning of maelstrom.

The death certificate recorded that he suffered 'bruising and oedema of the brain, associated with fractures of the skull and a blow on the left side of the head'.

*

The army raided the house during the wake, searching for Paddy who, they presumed, would have risked sneaking into Derry for the funeral. They came at two in the morning, and searched all the rooms, including the room where the coffin lay. They invigilated mourners. They didn't notice Pio who was wanted by the police. The family telephoned local curate Fr Lackin, who came and persuaded the soldiers to leave. Peggy was given three valium tablets to calm her down. She went, heavily sedated, to the cemetery next day. Margie miscarried her baby during the funeral.

Peggy had needed a lot of money in a hurry to meet the cost of daily family visits to Michael in Belfast, followed by the costs of his funeral. She solved it in her usual fashion by applying for subs to her solicitor. The Department of the Environment had agreed to pay her £800 compensation for a fall into a Bogside pothole and her solicitor lent her money out of his own pocket until the award should come through.

During Michael's illness and death, from 10 March until 19 March, he gave Peggy sums totalling exactly £800, the receipts for which she kept. She also kept the printed invitations to Michael's wedding, and the condolence notices on his death which were printed in the local newspaper.

She used to read these in Michael's bedroom, to which she transferred and where she now spent most of her time, lying on the single bed, her head resting against the wall, exactly as Michael's head had rested against that end of the coffin which had rested against that same wall.

She slept and ate and sang there, crooning endlessly her own adaptation of a country-and-western lament:

> From the day he left the world
> He's been mammy's little boy,
> He's my Michael,
> I'm his mammy,
> And he's mine.

The marks on the wall above where Necky used lay his sleeping head, showed how deeply this troubled woman had dug her fingernails into the plaster. She did not leave the house until Michael's fiancée gave birth to Michaela. The baptism of Peggy's granddaughter, in a church in a remote valley in Donegal, commanded full attendance of the Deery clan, including aunts and uncles and nieces and nephews.

Peggy then resumed, intermittently, cooking of her fabulous Sunday dinners. Paddy sometimes sneaked over the border and back into town to take his place at the table, so that she could count the numbers of all her surviving children and assure herself that they were alive and healthy, if not entirely safe. Pio had put her trust in fate, and police apathy, and moved her husband and children from Donegal back into Derry to live in her mother's house. Helen left her wanted husband in Donegal and squatted with her children into a house near her mother.

After Sunday dinner Peggy's children and grandchildren would follow her upstairs and into Michael's bedroom. They spent hours at a time sitting with her, piling the grand-children in on top of her. She refused to come downstairs during the week. She drew up lists of messages that the presses might remain stocked against further disaster: '1 lb.

butter, 2 packets fish fingers, 1 lb. tomatoes, 4 packets cheese, 6 toilet rolls, 2 tins peas, 2 tins beans, 2 tins tomatoes, load of bread.'

The phone became a life-support, a means of cajoling her to the foot of the stairs to hear from her daughters and sons, wherever they might be, whatever they might be doing. Spring turned to summer and summer turned to autumn and Paddy was caught and jailed in Belfast and refused bail. Peggy came downstairs again. The family took her on a gambling spree, says Helen. 'Uncle Buddy, or Uncle Mickey, took us all around in a mini-van. We paid twenty pence each for the petrol. We played bingo every night. We went to Buncrana on Tuesday, the Bogside on Wednesday, the Metric in Burnfoot on Thursday, Derry again on Friday, Saturday at the poker machines, Buncrana on Sunday, and Monday on the poker machines.'

Peggy gambled and lost on compensation for Michael's death. She rejected a settlement from the government, opting for a civil suit against the owner of the discotheque. He left the country, leaving unpaid bills behind.

Sandra tried forlornly to entice Peggy back to the happiness they had known. She wrote her a note, and sent it up with one of her children:

Now Peggy,
X said last night that he misses you and loves you and I brought it up about your needing some money. He said: 'Poor Peggy's health is not the best,' and I said Peggy is not only not well but she is getting a lot of things up the teeth at one time between one thing and another. I said to him maybe you could help her as she needs some money, and he said he was sympathetic but he couldn't do anything this week about it. That's all the news for now,
love,
Sandra.

Peggy refused to be drawn. She never set foot in another pub or dancehall or restaurant. She never went to the match-making festival in Lisdoonvarna, Co. Clare, in the Republic, where American cowboys were making annual visits and showing women how to barbecue steaks. Sick at heart, Peggy stayed with her children in the landscape of war.

*

One of the young men involved in the brawl with Necky was later killed in a car crash. Two were given an eighteen-month sentence for assaulting him. Upon release, they went to England.

Lobster, Crab and Salmon

Pio

Peggy's family haemorrhaged out of Derry into Donegal as the war continued. Paddy was followed by Johnny and Pio, each seeking refuge in the Republic from the British Army and the RUC. They lived in makeshift lodgings and mobile homes. It was Helen who found real peace there, and founded a real home there. She felt less hunted; it was her husband Seamus who was on the Northern wanted list. As the years passed, they both felt accepted south of the border.

They settled in a council house in the remote cliffside fishing village of Glengad. The younger Deerys frequently joined her and they too established their own connections with the village. Michael, had he lived, was to marry a young woman from there. Martin met his wife there. June married a man from there.

Before the North was divided by a border from the Republic, such connections were inevitable and natural. Donegal was the trading hinterland of Derry; there was a profitable co-mingling of agriculture and commerce; from the thriving port of Derry the produce of Donegal was shipped to Scotland, England and Wales. Intermarriage between the people of both counties was common.

Partition put an end to this intercourse. The port shut down gradually and commercial traffic from Donegal skirted the border, avoiding the North. Derry was forced to turn its back on Donegal and the rest of the Republic, and face into the Unionist stronghold of the six separated counties. The cultural, economic and political divide between North and South deepened to the point where the people of Derry and Donegal no longer cohabited as natural allies.

The relationship between former neighbours, though civil enough, became distinctly uneasy as the North plunged into war. Initial sympathy turned to fear and hostility as Donegal found itself playing host first to genuine refugees from Derry, then to hundreds of Northern IRA volunteers on the run. The mutual spleen ebbed and flowed in direct proportion to the action taken against the IRA by the Irish police and army. The ground rules were gradually established. At first, Northern IRA members were treated with something approaching historical compassion. Men found in possession of guns in the vicinity of Buncrana were given suspended sentences in 1970 by a judiciary which counselled restraint but also agreed not to publish their Northern addresses lest such identification be used by the British authorities to the men's 'detriment'. Seven men found in possession of a machine-gun 'seemed decent enough to the guards' said one State-prosecution solicitor. As the war dragged on, causing death in the Republic, attitudes soured. IRA volunteers caught in action, smuggling armaments or using Donegal as a base from which to attack the North, were subjected to the punitive process of Irish law. Volunteers who observed the law were kept under scrutiny and otherwise left alone. The Republic provided dole and jobs and housing.

The harsh re-education was a two-way process. At every turn, conscience snagged on reality. Donegal people learned at first hand the rigours of life in the North; Northerners came to appreciate the joy of living in a county at peace, and the tactical advantages of leaving it so.

Nevertheless, a period of penance had to be undergone before any refugee Northerner could make a home in Donegal. This usually took the form of grudging shelter in slum accomodation, while the authorities tested the *bona fides* of the newcomers. It was often impossible to know if a Northerner come among them was an active volunteer, an ex-volunteer, a genuine refugee from injustice, or someone who was simply fed up with the war.

*

Helen's husband Seamus scarcely knew his own status when he fled into Donegal in 1981. He and Johnny were on a laundry run, driving Paddy's van for him, when the IRA set up an ambush using the van as cover. In the ensuing gunbattle with soldiers, a bystander was killed. Seamus and Johnny fled across the border, convinced that the RUC would not believe that they had been, as they were, innocently working at the time.

Helen joined Seamus after two months in Donegal. A succession of makeshift homes followed. The couple and their two children lived in a mobile home on the wind-swept cliffs of Malin Head, then in a caravan on a beach in Buncrana, and then in a rented thatched house in Burnfoot, near the Derry border. From this house Seamus went one day to buy a bottle of milk. The Irish police picked him up for questioning and he was held for forty-eight hours. He was glad to get back to the cottage though it had no electricity or running water or indoor toilet; it was home. 'The rain,' says Helen, 'used to drip into the kitchen. On a really bad day, I'd have to sweep the water out of the living-room. We spent that year in wellington boots.' But it was home, and it was peaceful, and they were alive and they were healthy and the family life she lived there with her husband and children was as far removed from her past as it was possible to be.

On Bloody Sunday, when she was thirteen, Helen lay on the ground as the bullets whizzed overhead, crying out: 'I want my mammy.' Then she walked around looking at the dead bodies, looking for her mother. The soldiers camped behind her home were a baleful presence. 'They'd lift you into the back of the pig, the jeep, using their knees to push you inside. It was all men and a big dog inside. Me mammy always went up to the camp after us, and she'd sit in their waiting-room. In the street they'd make us open our coats so they could look at us, checking us for guns. I used to be that embarrassed, my eyes would fill up. One day I said no, no more. They said they were bringing me to the camp. Me mammy came flying along the street, pushing herself on her two walking sticks, and said she wasn't having me lifted any more, so she pulled open my coat for them. Then she beat me home with her two sticks.'

Helen married Seamus when she was twenty and they spent the first year of their married life in Peggy's house, sharing the three-bedroom home with Peggy, Johnny, Owney, Pio, May, Bridie, Kathleen, Tony, Michael, Martin, June and Bernadette. By the age of twenty-two she was with Seamus in Donegal.

She was happy there. Helen has imbibed her mother's cheerful approach to life, family and home: 'Wherever you are, if you've tea-bags, sugar and plenty of spuds, you can never go wrong. Make sure it's an eight-stone bag of spuds.' She discovered another life resource, turf, which lay there for the digging and burning in the bogs of Donegal. Wherever she was, Helen enjoyed looking out the window of her kitchen and seeing a solid stack of turf piled against the wall. It meant the family would never be cold.

*

In their Donegal odyssey they met people they would not have otherwise met. Seamus befriended an English couple, with no visible means of support, who lived in a tent alongside their mobile home. He says, 'I was so fucking sorry for them in their tent. I offered them stew out of our pot. Me and him started walking into town then.' Town was Malin, a small village one and a half miles from their mobile. As Helen grew more pregnant, the journey proved too much.

When the offer of a council house in Glengad came through, Helen felt her life touched by magic. The remote village is tucked into a fold in the mountains, above the Atlantic ocean, with majestic views of land and sea. Derry was a skilled hour's drive away. The church was nearby, a short run in the mini-bus which collected the faithful every Sunday morning. There was turf to spare, and lobster, salmon and crabs to eat when Seamus got seasonal work on a half-decker plying out of the tiny harbour.

Helen took up reading, and knitting and baking. She read all the works of Walter Macken, and began to study Irish history. She taught herself intricate Icelandic knitting patterns, producing eleven fishermen's sweaters in twelve weeks. She mastered the Aga cooker, and fed her family and visitors with fresh bread, scones and cakes. 'The first time I used the oven was a disaster. I made rock buns. We ended up throwing them at each other in the field, pretending to have a riot. Some of us were British soldiers. Some of us were the Deery family.'

Helen's third child was born in Donegal, as gentle a rite of passage into the county as could be hoped for.

When Michael was killed, Helen returned abruptly to Derry to squat into a house in Creggan and devote herself to her mother. The grim roundabout of gambling, on which she embarked with Peggy and the others, took its toll. Helen stopped when her children began to fret. 'It wasn't fair on them, or even the wee babysitter, seven nights a week.' Seamus, stranded in Donegal, occupied himself by drinking with Paddy. One night he and Paddy found themselves on the wrong side of the border. The RUC arrested them.

Charges against Seamus of withholding information on the laundry van were eventually dropped, but the time spent in jail, on remand, meant an effective end to their life in the Republic. Helen, uncertain that Seamus would ever get out of prison, relinquished tenancy of their house in Glengad.

They live now, legal tenants, in a house in the street below where Peggy lived. Their three children, aged eight and under, show no traces of a life lived in the Republic. The youngest is the butt of bitter-sweet jokes – the first member of the Deery clan to have been born a free person, in the Free State.

*

Pio, Peggy's third-eldest daughter, lived as close to the border and to Derry as was possible during her exile in Donegal. A ten minute stroll would have brought her into the North. Like Helen, she returned home to Peggy when Necky was killed. She lives now with her husband and six children in a spanking new housing estate in Ballymagroarty on the outskirts of Derry. The estate nestles right up against the border with Donegal. Pio leaves Ballymagroarty nearly every day, to travel back up to Creggan by taxi to see her sisters and brothers. The people of her estate have not yet established an identity. They are not of the city; nor do they belong to the agricultural society at their back-door. The names given to streets in Ballymagroarty reflect the cultural and political aspirations of the nationalist majority on Derry city council. Where once Unionists named streets inhabited by Catholics after military heroes of the British Empire – Wellington, Blucher, Nelson – the current names evoke the literary and musical achievements of the Irish. Raftery is a poet, O'Riada a composer, Friel is a playwright.

Pio is firmly established as a mother. She likes this career very much. She came to it early, 'teaching me ma to walk. Margie used to take the calipers from her, and stand beside her, and I'd be a couple of steps away saying, "Come on, Mammy, you can do it. You can walk."' She was eleven when she saw her mother take the first faltering steps again.

Pio was sacked for bad time-keeping shortly after starting her first job in a denim factory. She used to get sick in the morning, going down the lane, and she frequently missed the factory bus. No one noticed that she was pregnant. She was a chubby eighteen-year-old.

One Tuesday morning she got up to join her mother and Helen in the housework and felt extremely ill. She did not wish to admit that she had a stomach-ache, lest Peggy ask questions and find out her secret. She pleaded a headache and went back to bed. She did not come downstairs for the midday meal. Helen brought up her dinner and complained at her laziness, which she thought was an excuse not to have to wash the windows. Pio said she wasn't hungry and asked if she could have a cigarette. She heard Helen speak to her mother, and then Peggy came to the foot of the stairs and called up: 'No eats, no fags.' Pio responded: 'Ma, come on up quick, on your own.'

Peggy went upstairs. She saw that Pio had given birth. Her mother asked her if the afterbirth had come away. Pio didn't know what she was talking about. Her mother made her lie back on the bed again, and started pushing her stomach. She pushed three times and the afterbirth came out. Pio thinks the effort of jumping out of bed, after the shock of the birth, must have broken the umbilical cord. She had felt no pain whatsoever. In hospital she had to be given three sutures. The nurses called her 'wonderwoman'.

Her biggest worry that night was what Paddy would say 'It was him I was panicking on. He used to come home every evening and ask where I'd been. I was afraid he'd kill me.' Peggy threatened to kill her when she had recovered.

Since that day Pio has been a fulltime mother. On one of her frequent jaunts across the border with her mother, to see Paddy, Johnny or Helen, Pio met her future husband Tom, a native of Donegal. He was a farm labourer. She liked him but cast a cold city eye on his rural appearance. 'He was an antique – he wore bell-bottoms in 1981.' As the relationship deepened, and gifts were exchanged at Christmas, Peggy bought him his first pair of fashion trousers, and Pio bought him his first pair of what she termed 'groovy shoes'. These were the things that mattered, not the fact that he was of the Protestant faith. Tom is one of eleven children. He adopted the Catholic faith when the time came to marry Pio. They met in August, were engaged in December, and married the following year, setting up home in a two-bedroomed council flat in Creggan.

*

Pio's second child was six weeks old in December 1982 when the police came at dawn to take her away, citing Sections 11 and 12 of the Terrorism Act. A Derryman, and member of the IRA, called Raymond Gilmour had turned Queen's evidence to save himself from jail, and had named more than thirty people, including Pio, in his confession. This phenomenon of mass-trial on the word of an informer, with no supporting evidence, became known in the North as 'supergrass'.

As Pio dressed and prepared herself to be taken away, she heard Tom ask the police which station he should ring if he wanted to enquire what was happening to her. 'I heard them say Castlereagh, and my knees started knocking. You know the way it is – you hear people talking about there and your imagination works overtime.' Castlereagh is infamous in Northern folklore as an interrogation centre. There have been documented cases of torture of police suspects there; under emergency powers, people can be detained in Castlereagh for seven days, without charge or access to relatives.

Pio was taken in a police jeep, under army escort, from Creggan, at six in the morning, down to the army base, Fort George. There she was placed in a car with two policemen and one policewoman, and taken to Castlereagh, on the outskirts of Belfast. She signed a statement within hours, confessing to the withholding of information about the IRA. 'I never signed nobody else away. I only signed myself into a charge though they kept me there for three days.' Paddy had often told her that they'd probably bring her in for questioning someday, on account of him, and that they would persuade her to sign anything, such would be her fear. She is proud that she only incriminated herself.

Pio was taken from Castlereagh to Armagh Women's Prison, where she was lodged in a cell on her own. There were two other Derrywomen on remand in Armagh Jail, also charged on the word of the two Derry supergrasses, Raymond Gilmour and Robert Quigley. One of them, Cathy Moore, refused to allow prison warders to strip-search her and her resistance led to daily tension in the prison. The warders forcibly stripped her. 'When it came Cathy's turn, the screws would lock us in wherever we were that day, in the kitchen or the TV room, and we'd hear them fight and carry Cathy all the way to the strip section. Then she'd be punished for resisting and she'd spend her time in lock-up, in solitary.'

Pio spent her time in the cell, or in the communal kitchen and TV room. Remand prisoners were allowed to receive food and fruit from visitors to supplement the jail diet, and she whiled away the hours washing her clothes or cooking meals. She disliked, intensely, the chamber pot in her cell. She wrote every day to Tom and to Peggy.

Her solicitor assured her that she had a good chance of beating the charge and the confession, on the grounds of post-natal depression. 'I signed when the baby was six weeks old. The minute they said to me that the children would be taken into care, that a man wouldn't be allowed to rear them, I signed.' Pio's confidence faltered when her application for bail was refused.

Helen and Bridie were in court when her second application was heard. She had been one month in Armagh Jail. The judge released her to a family homecoming where celebrations were such that she was sorely tempted to get drunk except that: 'I hate drink. I detest it. If I'm out in company, and people drink a lot, I get bored.' Peggy had plenty to celebrate: a daughter released from prison, and Michael due to finish his sentence in weeks.

There was another reason why Pio did not whole-heartedly join the celebrating throng that night. Upon release, she found that she had grown to detest any company at all. After a lifetime of living in the bosom of a large and noisy family, and moving directly from that into a family unit with Tom, Pio had discovered the unexpected pleasures of solitude and privacy in a room of her own, albeit in prison. 'I was that used to quietness, I couldn't stick the wains crying. I couldn't stick crowds. I had gotten used to doing nothing and seeing nobody from eight at night till eight in the morning. It took me ages to adjust.'

It was a condition of bail that she had to report to the RUC, down at the city barracks, once a week, and promise not to leave the jurisdiction. This meant she could not travel into Donegal. It meant she had to stay quiet under the utmost provocation, should a policeman be inclined when she signed on to make a jibe about her mother. 'They would call her chicken-leg. I hated that. Or they'd ask how one-eye was, meaning Paddy.'

*

As the date of trial drew near, Pio was informed that she was to face a further, far more serious charge, of intent to endanger life. This both frightened and annoyed her. 'I'm loyal to Paddy, but I wouldn't hurt a fly.' She decided to leave the jurisdiction permanently. It was a simple thing to do. In the spring of 1983 she got on one of the many buses that travel daily from Derry to Buncrana, crowded with trippers or Donegal people returning home from a day's shopping. Tom travelled over later that day, legally and unhindered, with the children. They moved into a mobile home, stationed in the garden of the council house where Tom's parents live.

Close as she was to the border, Pio didn't feel that she was living in a different country. She felt that she was living in an arcadian extension of Derry, with none of its wartime problems. She returned to Creggan on a weekly, sometimes daily basis, swimming through the security dragnet as easily as a minnow through a shark-net. The soldiers and the police, with their armoured cars and tanks and guns and helicopters were conducting a war. Pio was doing her shopping.

'I started coming in gradually on the shoppers' bus. Tom's relatives and all the people of the area were going every Friday night to Derry in these fleets of buses, to stock up with bargains. The price difference was enormous between the Free State and the North. You could save twenty pounds on a week's groceries for the price of a twenty-minute bus ride.' As her confidence increased, so did the frequency of her visits, until she started travelling on the day-trips, bringing her children with her. There was an impregnable sense of safety in Creggan, where word of mouth about the encroachment of soldiery travelled faster than the lumbering convoy in which they were forced to travel. Frequent change of regiment every four months meant, in any case, that the soldiers, strangers in a strange land, would hardly know who they were supposed to be looking for, and the Deery sisters were by now adept at changing names with each other. 'I'm not Pio. I'm Margie', [or Helen, or Bridie, or May or Bess or Bernadette].

Pio missed her mother very much. Peggy came rarely to the caravan to visit them. 'You'd have to offer dinner to her, like setting a lure. She loved getting her dinner handed to her.' The lure was not strong enough to entice her totally. 'Me ma was never one for visiting in another person's home. She was only ever comfortable in her own. And she hated walking down the country road with a limp. She imagined everybody noticed it and passed remarks on it.'

*

When Michael was injured, and transferred to Belfast, Pio spent the week in Derry waiting for news. She was still officially on the run, and couldn't risk the trip through the entire North. When Michael died Peggy said to Pio, 'Stay with me,' and Pio, seven months pregnant, cast caution to the winds and moved her family back to Derry. Most of the supergrass trials and appeals had in any case formally collapsed, including hers. Convictions had been overturned upon appeal, and many of those who had signed confessions and fled trial were given to understand that the police might not try to hold their own words against them. In Pio's case it proved to be so. After three years exile, she was back where her mother thought she belonged, in Derry. The family home now housed Peggy, Kathleen, May and her baby, Martin, June and her baby, Bernadette, Pio and Tom and their four children.

Pio stayed until the baby was born and then she squatted into a nearby house, fixed up the sitting-room and kitchen, and carpeted the ground floor. When she eventually accepted legal tenancy of a house in Ballymagroarty, where most people were loath to go, the house she vacated was squatted into by Owney and his wife and their new baby. Expenses for the furbishment of Pio's new, much bigger home were met by an intricate piece of financial juggling. The cooker and carpets which she had bought on hire-purchase instalment were left with Owney in exchange for a suitable sum. Owney had just been paid compensation by the Department of the Environment for injuries sustained in an accident in Creggan. To Owney's cash was added money from a similar compensation claim by Pio, which had also just been paid. It was processed through the court though she had been on the run and on the wanted list at the time of hearing. Small financial claims are rushed through Northern courts as the authorities try to keep the judicial conveyor belt free for political trials.

Physical manifestations of stress are evident in Pio's family. She and two of her six children suffer from eczema. She resists the temptation to play the one-armed bandits too frequently. She knows there is no profit to be gained from slotting coins into a fruit-machine and mechanically pulling the lever for hours at a time, but she is quite clear about the soporific benefits. It's better than drinking; or popping pills; and: 'It lifts your mind off everything. You stop thinking. After Necky died, me ma wouldn't come out to dance. It was the dancing I loved, going onto the floor with her. When she was crippled, I never thought I'd be out to dance with her one day.'

Pio would like an education for her children. 'Nowadays you need A-levels and O-levels to work, if there was work. In my time, you didn't really need that. I learned as much as I had to. I can read when I have to read. I can read well enough to do me. I can read the death notices in the paper. I've read enough of them to do me for the rest of my life.'

The Bungling Gang

Johnny

Johnny was twelve years old when his mother was shot. He stopped going to school. When she was returned to Altnagelvin Hospital from Belfast, he went every day to see her. Each morning he walked down the hill into town, to the bus station. If he had the fare, he paid it. If not, he opened the door to the luggage compartment, crawled in, closed the door and got out at the hospital terminus.

He spent the whole day in the hospital. He washed his mother's underwear in the sink, every day, her knickers and her bra, and her nightdress, and left the clothes on the radiator to dry. He shared her food. If the matron was around during mealtimes, he hid in the linen cupboard in the corridor and a nurse brought his dinner to him. He understood that his mother would spend the rest of her life in bed. That she would never walk again.

At night he returned to Creggan and joined in the riots against the soldiers. He was better equipped than most to fight them because he knew their ways and their methods. Before his mother was shot, Johnny had been adopted by them as a mascot.

He was ten years old when the British Army first arrived in the city. He used to visit them in their makeshift camps, particularly the billets in the city centre. He ran messages for them, going to shops to buy their chocolate, and soft drinks and comic-cuts. They gave him money for this. He was rich, for a boy, and they gave him the run of the camps as he became known to them. The British Army bases became his adventure playgrounds. It was a soldier who first taught Johnny to strip and clean and oil a gun. If he stayed late at the camps, the soldiers who had to patrol Creggan would give him a lift home in the jeep. One night the soldiers went into his house to say hello to his parents. Next day, he said, the soldiers came back and brought food into the house. There were big tins of corned beef and cartons of canned fruit.

They called in regularly with food after that. At one camp, in a disused bus station, where Johnny was a particular favourite, the soldiers collected money and presented him with a pair of shoes. Then they dressed him in a miniature soldier's outfit. He remembers the sweater. It was green. It was warm. A picture of him in the boy-soldier's outfit appeared in a newspaper. This happiness continued for a long time. He doesn't remember exactly when things changed but he remembers the day he decided that he wouldn't be going back to the camps any more. The people had been fighting the soldiers in the streets over internment. Johnny had been stealing the occasional bullet from the camps and giving the bullets to the Official IRA who operated from a shop near his home.

He knew it was time to change sides. On that last day, Johnny decided to capitalise on his earning power. He went round all the camps with his younger brother Owney, collecting lists from the soldiers of the messages they wanted, and the money with which to purchase the goods. He thinks they may have got around twenty pounds. He disappeared up into Creggan, behind the barricades, with the cash, and never went voluntarily back into the camps again.

*

Johnny became a rioter, throwing stones at the soldiers. They continued coming to his home, but they never again brought gifts. They brought search warrants, arrest warrants, and all the repressive regalia of an army at war.

Johnny, for his part, rose swiftly through the ranks of a people at war. It was unpaid work, but it was, for a child, dangerously thrilling. The normal rules of life did not apply. He could tear up pavements and loot building sites for supplies to build a barricade and there was no reprimand; children learned to play tennis with tear-gas grenades and rubber bullets, expertly batting them back to the troops; they were allowed to get up out of bed in the middle of the night and go into the streets when the bin-lids sounded a warning that the soldiers were trying to invade the area.

He learned to drive a car. Many children did, as the vigilantes hijacked vehicles for emergency runs around Free Derry.

Then his father died and his mother was shot and Paddy was blinded and the adventures came to an end. Life was sad and rough and bitter. Johnny turned to crime.

He robbed things and burgled shops. 'Never houses. It would be wrong to rob people.' He is not proud of that now, and scarcely refers to it, preferring to concentrate instead on the vaguely political acts for which he served time in jail, but his behaviour was adjudged by his community as anti-social. In the absence of normal social structures and formal policing of the area, people brought their complaints to the

Provisional IRA, and demanded retribution. It was demanded that Johnny be punished.

The fact that Paddy was by now a fully fledged member of the IRA, and on the run, and in danger, ensured punishment rather than clemency for Johnny. The IRA had to be seen to disavow favouritism. Paddy's best friend can still remember what happened when the IRA set out to punish the boy.

'We used to go to Peggy's every day, even when we were on the run. The day they went for Johnny, we hadn't the nerve to turn up at her house. They sent the wrong man for him. This man's sister had gone off with a British soldier and Peggy stood at the door and told the street about it as he took Johnny away. The man would be better off fetching his sister home than taking her child away, she said. There was a terrible row. Everybody felt rotten.'

Johnny's head was shaved. He came home with a bare skull, which marked him as an outsider in the community.

Paddy and his friend returned to Peggy's home after a few days, dreading her anger. 'But she just smiled and growled and said, "Sit down there to your dinner." In a way she was relieved. She wanted something done about Johnny because he had gone out of control and she knew he would end up in jail for a crime. That would be the worst thing. Jail was bad, but to go there as a criminal would be shameful.'

The police did catch up with Johnny, and he was jailed for stealing cars. He was remanded in Crumlin Jail, without bail, and then sentenced to the borstal wing of the H-Blocks for sixteen months. In borstal he faked a suicide attempt, injuring himself severely and was transferred to Magilligan Prison, where 'I done the whole time in hospital'. He insists that the suicide attempt wasn't serious. 'You call it doing the beef. It means you slit your arms, or some people eat light bulbs, and then they make you do your time in the hospital wing.'

Peggy took it seriously. Her son had a haunted, lost quality. He often referred to the fact he was one of twins, and that the other twin had died in the womb. He said he would kill himself if ever she died. When his brothers and sisters talk of him they say 'Johnny . . .' in a specially affectionate, hopeless kind of way. Peggy feared his wild rages.

*

Johnny and his friends formed a kind of outriders group to the disbanded members of the Official IRA who had gone on to form another paramilitary organisation called the Irish National Liberation Army. The INLA veered between gangsterism and warfare, and the outriders offered them safe houses, and kept their weaponry for them. It was understood that the outriders could occasionally use the guns for their own criminal activities.

'We called ourselves the People's Liberation Army, but we were just a bunch of hoods,' says Johnny now. When they were finally caught, the judge referred to them as a 'bungling gang'. Johnny uses that term when describing himself during that era. It takes the hard edge off activities of which he is now not proud. It puts his teenage years into soft focus – 'the bungling gang'.

When Johnny and his friend were caught, they confessed almost immediately. A police note of the interrogation of Johnny, made available to the court during his trial, says:

> He was agitated and disturbed and said that if he was charged he would not leave the police station alive. He jumped up and down and struck his head against the door. Accused started to cry and began to shake. He got off the chair and screamed, running towards the wall.

Johnny's partner related in a statement to the police just how the 'bungling gang' went about their business:

> I met Johnny Deery and I went to his house and started talking about doing a job, about doing the Credit Union or Creggan Post Office. We were talking about another place out the Buncrana Road. I said we broke into it one time before. I stayed all night in Johnny's house and me and Johnny got up at 6 a.m. and I went over to my house and knocked my mother to get in. I went up the stairs and into my bedroom and opened the window and put my hand out to the drainpipe and lifted down a .45 revolver and took it

into my bedroom. I went to my wardrobe and lying at the back of my clothes in a perfume box I got five rounds of .45s. I put the bullets in my pocket and the gun in my waistband and slipped out the back-door and right over to Johnny's.

Johnny's statement says that then:

> We left the house together and X took the gun with him. It is not his gun, it belongs to the INLA and he takes it with him to defend himself and to do the odd job. We went towards Milanda Bakery. X saw a breadvan and he decided he was going to rob it. I was to stand across the street and watch for anyone coming and he was to go to the back of the breadvan when the doors were open and take the money off the man, using the gun. I was to make sure nobody would come across and catch us. He told me what he was doing and the breadvan pulled away. He followed it to see where it was going. X followed the breadvan and it went up the Northlands Avenue and he decided he was going to rob it. I told him to go up to Northlands Crescent, the Avenue was too chancy and I told him he might get caught.'

An army patrol arrived, and X gave the gun to Johnny and Johnny threw it into a garden, knocked on a door, said he was on the run, and walked through the house into a backyard. Later he came back and retrieved the gun. The army came back and picked up him and X.

Among other charges made as a result of confessions, Johnny was charged with possession of a firearm on 15 November 1978. He was then nineteen years old. During a year's remand in Crumlin Jail he injured himself again, and was transferred to Long Kesh where he again sustained such self-inflicted wounds that he was transferred to the prison hospital.

He still insists that he was merely 'doing the beef'. He would have done anything to get out of a prison cell. 'I hated it. I couldn't do time. Locked up, then something goes wrong and they put you on the boards, in a cell with no mattress, no pillow, just a blanket on the floor. They strip you naked, men in white coats, and put you into a padded cell after a whack in the stomach and them all round you, beating you. You could crack up.'

Johnny used warn his mother when she visited him that he was 'going to do it tonight'. The visits were traumatic for them both. If he bungled, he would die. Johnny enlisted Peggy's help. He explained to her the various categories of suicide attempts. If he slashed his arm from wrist to shoulder with a Stanley knife, prison officers would record that he had tried to kill himself, and recommend hospital. If he merely scratched his skin with a pin, the officers would make a similar recommendation. Peggy used to give Johnny pins. The longer he stayed in prison, the more often and more deeply he had to score his skin with the pins. Johnny's arms are permanently welted from wrist to elbow. Peggy did not visit him often. She hated seeing her son in prison, could hardly bear to help him hurt himself, worried that Johnny might be driven to take his own life. Conditions in Long Kesh were so horrific that other men were already pondering the option of starving themselves to death.

Nevertheless, says Johnny, he never seriously contemplated suicide. If anything, he is embarrassed at how often he bungled his fake attempts. He is good at telling stories against himself. 'I woke up in the hospital ward in Long Kesh at two in the morning and said to myself: "Fuck, I'm going to do it." I moved the TV to the centre of the floor, stood on a chair, hung the TV cable over a rafter, wrapped it round my neck and jumped. When I landed on the floor, on both feet, I knew something had gone wrong.'

He felt, in fact, very comfortable for a man who was supposed to be hanging himself. He looked behind and saw about two yards of cable dragging on the floor. It hung from his neck, from the rafter, from everywhere, like tinsel you'd see on a Christmas tree. It was a very long cable indeed.

He had to move quickly to restore order before the warder came by on his rounds. It was difficult to move quickly because he was strung out on Largactyl, Merlin and Roche tranquillisers. 'I could hardly lift a box of matches, never mind all that cable.'

After some months in the prison hospital, Johnny got really depressed. 'I was browned off. So I'd light a cigarette and burn the tattoo off my arm, bit by bit.' The tattoo had disappeared before Johnny was finally set free.

Before release, there was one last ordeal, in court. 'The Judge gave the first guy fourteen years and started running along the queue, giving ten years, twelve years. There were eight of us in the dock. He let one fellow off with a suspended sentence, then he came to me and I was panicking. There was a doctor speaking about my backgound, about me mother being shot, and me father dying, and I said to meself: "Oh, Jesus." I was ready to drop. Here's me, facing him, and he was saying he was not going to send me to prison, I'd have to go to hospital, to Gransha, all that crack, and he gave me two years suspended for three years, or something, I don't remember, fuck me, I nearly fainted.' He was then transferred to open custody in Gransha Mental Hospital in Derry.

There is a lot Johnny does not remember about the seventies, the decade of his teenage years. His conversation is a seamless recall of riots, prisons, and hospitals. It was during his stay in the mental hospital that he got his first, last and only legitimate job, at the age of twenty. The doctors had allowed him to go home from Thursday night until Tuesday morning and he met a girl and they had a love affair. The manager of the factory where she worked sent for Johnny, and offered to help. He gave Johnny a job and Johnny quit the hospital. He bought the young girl an engagement ring out of his wages. It cost eighty pounds. The doctors came along then and told Johnny the situation was hopeless. If it came to the attention of the courts that Johnny was well enough to work, they would say he was well enough for prison. Johnny left the job, and returned to hospital intermittently. The engagement was broken off.

*

He was released back into the community in 1981 and onto the dole. He qualified for permanent sickness benefit, the medical assessment of his condition. Johnny decided to start a new life in England. He went over on the boat and was immediately arrested under the Prevention of Terrorism Act. This act allows police in Britain to detain suspects for questioning, without charge, for a maximum period of seven days. It allows them to deport a suspect, without charge or appeal, back to Ireland, North or South. It allows them to ban suspects from Northern Ireland, who are British subjects, from ever returning to Britain. The police released Johnny, without charge or deportation after twenty-four hours. He went to stay with his aunt, in Wakefield. Every time he heard an Englishman hail somebody in the street, with the familiar 'Oi, you there', Johnny jumped, thinking soldiers were after him. He made a reverse-charge call to Coleraine in Northern Ireland, to his former parish priest from Creggan, and asked for help. The priest sent him the air-fare and Johnny left England eight days after he arrived in it.

He stayed with the priest in Coleraine, and helped to paint the youth hall. At night in the pubs he met young Protestants who were as lost as himself. They swapped prison stories. The priest trusted Johnny to count the money offered during Sunday mass, of which fact Johnny is unconscionably proud. After a fortnight of this hospitality, Johnny returned to Derry a new man. He met and settled down with a woman and they started a family.

He decided to help his brother Paddy work a laundry run, collecting bedclothes from Creggan for delivery to the laundry run by an order of nuns. When the van was hijacked from him by the IRA, a rifle was taken out from under the dirty laundry and a gun-battle with British soldiers was engaged. Johnny, though innocent of involvement, deemed it prudent to go on the run in Donegal.

He was away for a year. Peggy eased the dilemma of financing her now numerous forays into another country in search of her children by claiming Johnny's disablement allowance for him in Derry, unknown to him.

*

Johnny took a job in a pub perched on an isolated mountain in Donegal.

'There was a three-bedroom house attached to the pub. It came with the job, fully furnished. It had a cooker and a big fireplace. Ann and me took turns tending the bar. People would come for a drink in the early afternoon and sit there till late in the evening, if they went home at all. They'd come in their tractors, even come in off the boats, call for the one drink and have a whole lot to drink. The man who was in charge of making sure people weren't working and collecting the dole at the same time used to come in and drink with people who were working and collecting the dole and drinking all at the one time.'

It was understood that the bar staff would stay until the customers decided it was time to go home. This decision might sometimes be taken at dawn. Johnny and Ann, working shifts, and looking after the baby, scarcely saw each other.

The pub-owner offered them a three-year lease on the premises. Small as the premises were, and isolated as they were, they afforded the prospect of profit. One day, as Johnny pondered the offer, the man with responsibility for collecting garbage on the mountain came in for a drink. It was mid-morning and the man ordered a bottle of stout. Johnny, sitting behind the bar, mentioned that his stomach couldn't settle. He felt as though there were butterflies in it. The man bought Johnny a brandy and port. Other men drifting in attested to its medicinal merit and bought Johnny one cure after another. 'By half past ten that night, I was happy as Larry and drunk as a skunk. I knew I had to just walk away from that job and I did, leaving the bar to the owner. The garbage collector was still there when I left.'

When they returned to Derry, Johnny asked Ann several times to marry him. On one occasion they applied to the Catholic Church authorities for letters of freedom which would allow them to formalise the relationship, but the letters were refused because she was young, and pregnant, and the priest was cautious. The birthrate in Derry among young single girls had increased alarmingly, as had the rate of marital breakdown.

On a more recent occasion, after the birth of their second child, Johnny applied again for a Church wedding. There was no reply. One morning, after Johnny had left his child to school, he saw his parish priest walking along the street. 'C'mere, ye fucker,' he said to the priest, 'I've been sitting waiting on ye in the house. Why didn't ye come to see us about the wedding?' The priest told him that he had been up to talk with the prospective bride. 'She doesn't want to marry you, Johnny.'

Ann is not yet willing to commit herself to Johnny in that formal way. He has a problem with drinking, she says. Johnny says there's little else to do. On nights when he has money, and an available car, he and his friends drive downtown and sit in the carpark, near the pubs. They buy a twenty-four-pack of lager for six pounds and mix it with cider to make a drink called snakebite. Towards closing time, if they have spare cash, they go into the pubs like any other citizen. If funds are particularly short, they take their cider and lager onto Derry's walls and drink it there with all the other people who can't afford to get in out of the cold. The walls are thronged on any given night.

Johnny maintains a close and antagonistic relationship with the police. He is regularly fined for motoring offences – driving while disqualified, taking and driving away somebody else's car, driving without insurance. On days when he is legitimately driving a relative's car, he can be done for dangerous driving or whatever the police come up with.

This mutually antagonistic relationship is a civil extension of the disturbances in the the town. It usually only occurs outside the Catholic ghetto areas, where the RUC have long abandoned any pretence at normal policing. There is one policeman who is personally known to Johnny. They address each other familiarly by first names. The name is usually preceded with an epithet.

Sometimes the police refuse to arrest Johnny at all. 'We'll

get you when we want you,' they say. They take him when relationships have reached needlepoint.

Ann and the children lived, until recently, in one house in Creggan, near the Deery family home, and Johnny lives in a nearby flat. Both homes were acquired by the process of squatting. If they were to marry, their income would drop drastically, as formally recognised relationships are given one, lesser, welfare payment.

*

The complex web of the relationship between Johnny and the statelet of Northern Ireland was illustrated in a bizarre way over a recent three-day period. On Monday, 21 March 1988, Johnny went to Ann's home and telephoned the police to see what action had been taken about allegations he had made of police assault upon his person. While Johnny sat talking in Ann's home, a joint police-army patrol were round the corner conducting a routine raid on his flat. They had burst the door open in order to effect entrance.

They acknowledged the damage done by scrawling the following words on the outside of a sealed brown envelope which was lying in Johnny's hallway:

These premises were searched by police on 21.3.88 at 7.30 p.m., by virtue of Section 15, NIEP (Northern Ireland Emergency Provisions) Act. Eily forced front door. This has been temporarily repaired. If further details are required, contact Strand Road RUC, Sgt. 11573.

This scrawl entitled Johnny to claim for repairs to his flat. The sealed envelope on which it was written contained a letter which the police had posted to Johnny. The letter informed him that he was due to be charged that Wednesday with illegal occupation of the flat:

The Magistrate's Court, (NI) Order 1981, article 20 (1) and (2): rule 8 of the Magistrate's Court Rules (NI) 1984. Summons to defendant to answer complaint at Petty Sessions District of Londonderry by NI Housing Exective.

> Whereas a complaint has been made before me that on the 12th day of October, you the said defendant, contrary to article 10 of the Criminal Justice (NI) Order 1986, with intent wrongfully to take possession of, or use, these premises, wrongfully entered such premises, this is to command you to appear on Wednesday, 23rd March, at 10.30 in the forenoon ...

Johnny picked up this letter on Tuesday 22 March. He also picked up another letter, again sent to him by the police:

> Re: the complaint against police made by you on 30 Dec, 1987. I refer to previous correspondence and your call of 21st March, 1988. I will be present at Strand Road RUC at 4 on Thursday, 24 March, 1988.
> Signed R. Colgan,
> Chief Inspector,
> Limavady 66797.

Raided on Monday, due to appear in court on Wednesday, and with an appointment to meet the police on Thursday, Johnny went to Ann's home on Tuesday to sort out his life by telephone. He had to ring his solicitor, and Inspector Colgan. While he was on the phone to Inspector Colgan, he heard shots ring out. He looked out his window and saw heavy police and army activity at a checkpoint nearby. He continued his conversation with the Inspector. Later he heard that a policeman had just been shot dead at the checkpoint. At least he had an alibi.

He now had a dilemma. He expected that his nearby flat would be routinely raided that Tuesday night. He might be taken away for questioning. He might then miss his court case the next day. Worse, he might fight with the patrol which raided his flat and end up with a six-month sentence for assault. If he didn't go to his own home, he'd be under suspicion anyway by the troops who found him missing two nights in succession. If he stayed the night at Ann's house, and the patrol came there, she might lose her allowance on the grounds of cohabitation.

The only gleam of comfort in this dilemma, as far as

Johnny could see, was that the policeman who had just been killed had been processing charges against Johnny, of alleged assault at a checkpoint some time previously.

In the event, Johnny did not go to court, nor to the police station to further process his own charge. Should things become urgent, they would all know where to get each other.

*

The hour before dawn is a bad time for Johnny. After Necky died, he was sitting in Ann's house, in the living-room. She had taken one child on an overnight visit to her relatives and Johnny was in charge of their five-year-old boy. It was half past four in the morning. The breakfast programmes on television had not yet started. He had finished the fifth can of lager and there was no alcohol in the house. 'I was just sitting there looking at Necky's card. I was tense. I took the heart tablets to slow down my heart. Then I took two bottles of medicine and eighty painkillers. I began to get palpitations. I took Panadol and then I brought the kid over to Helen's house.

'I said, "Gone watch the child." She sent for the ambulance. I was lying in casualty and I was well doped up and I didn't feel any worries. I kept going on to the doctor about needing a stitch, and the doctor said never mind the stitch, we're fighting for your life. The heartbeat was forty, then it went to seventy. They gave me an injection into the arm. I didn't have a care in the world. I knew I was half-dead. The psychiatrist came up and seen me.' On several occasions since then, Johnny has found himself in hospital receiving emergency treatment. His relatives counter the worry this causes with black humour. If Johnny were to jump into the river, they say, he would surface with two fish in his pocket. They warn him that some night, in his distress, he might do something that would actually kill him. He is aware of the danger. He thinks of his mother, he thinks of Necky, he starts to drink 'and I wonder when I start to drink what I'm going to end up doing to myself'. Like all the Deery men, he is profoundly lucky in his choice of a female partner.' Ann knows I'm useless without her. Who have I to turn to, only her?' Ann abandoned her home in Creggan one day, moved across the river, and settled into another council house in a mixed community. There is less tension there. Johnny visits her daily, and she returns daily to visit his family in Creggan. She misses the company, but not the war in the Creggan estate. She hopes the quiet life, across the river will eventually bring quietude of a sort to Johnny. When he stays overnight, on a visit to his children, she hears him praying. Always, no matter where he is, Johnny says his prayers before going to sleep. He prays for his family, for Ann's family, for himself and for her. He learned to pray in a monastery in Donegal, where he was sent on holiday after Peggy was shot. The other children spent the holiday in a house down the road.

*

Johnny carries with him, usually, the motability certificate for the British government-subsidised car and insurance for which his mother finally qualified as a disabled person in 1987. He points out with relish the list of patrons of this particular service for the disabled. The chief patron is 'Her Majesty, the Queen'. Other patrons include the Rt Hon. Margaret Thatcher, prime minister, and the leaders of all the British opposition parties. Johnny also carries the motability certificate for his uncle's car which Johnny is insured to drive. His uncle was permanently disabled in the Second World War, fighting on the British side.

These certificates, he says, handed out like confetti, are the sum of British political attitudes to the North.

Head-peace

Bernadette Devlin Deery
and Paddy's son Patrick at
Paddy's coffin

There were times when Peggy walked out of her house,
away from the mass of children. 'I'm away now. Don't any
of yous follow me. I need head-peace.' They loved that. They
loved the way she trusted them to run the house by themselves. They loved the certitude that their mother would be
back soon. The younger ones particularly loved it. They had
no memory of the days and nights when Peggy did not dare
to return to her marital home. Home, for them, was a place
where a mother always lived, to which her children always

returned, even after they had established homes and families of their own. Paddy and Johnny and Pio had always done so, even if they risked jail to do it. The younger ones cleaved to Peggy, staying as physically close to her as was possible even when their time came to establish homes of their own. Tony and Bridie got houses in the street where their mother lived. Owney and Martin squatted into the street below her. June returned to Peggy after a brief marriage. May and Bess and Bernadette never left her house. Children of their time, children of a war that has now lasted twenty years, children who are in their twenties and younger, they lead the normal, pocked, lives of war.

*

Owney walked out of the house once, just as his mother was wont to do. While he sought teenage head-peace in the flat where he squatted, Peggy sent him his dinner in a pressure cooker. Owney returned home, after a while. On the second day of his honeymoon, in 1985, he and Donna changed their plans to travel round Ireland, turned the car round and headed home. They were lonely for their families. Like Owney, Donna is also part of a large brood. She revels in the company of her twelve sisters and brothers. She still goes every day to her mother's house, to help prepare and eat dinner.

Owney would love a job to keep himself occupied. Donna asked him why he hadn't tried for one when he called into a small building site to cadge discarded lengths of timber for their garden fence. Owney said he couldn't bear the thought of being turned down, and the other workers pitying him as he walked away. 'It gets more and more embarrassing. If you ask everybody you meet for a job, they end up hating to see you come down the road. They feel just as bad as you do. So you paste this silly smile on your face and pretend everything's terrific.'

In the best of all possible worlds, Owney would like to be a gardener. He once grew an onion in a flower pot. Vegetable production used to be a prized skill in Derry. The best plot in the Bogside was attached to the police station. Then the station closed because there wasn't enough crime in the area to merit a fulltime corps of policemen. Owney's uncles remember stealing apples from the police orchard.

Donna teases Owney about his other skill, painting. She came home one night to find that he had painted the front doorstep a brilliant white. He had been worried that she might trip in the dark and hurt herself. In fact, says Donna, she often pinches herself to see how much pain she can take. If nothing else, this is good training for the occasions when the police and army raid the house. Owney had already got his training, when he was sent at the age of nineteen to a youth-offenders' centre.

The beating administered by an IRA punishment squad had failed to deter him and then the police caught him. The first thing the screw did was beat him round the prison cell while declaring: 'You can't beat the system.' Owney hid under the bed and looked at the man's big boots. The man insisted that Owney call him 'Sir', which Owney did. Owney learned to discipline his tongue. This enrages the police when they raid the house. They roar at him and shout 'You cocky cunt.' Owney is not interested in spending any more time under the bed.

The house into which he and Donna squatted reflects their yearning for peace and quietude and beauty. The suite of furniture was given to them as a wedding present by Donna's mother who has a part-time job. The fan-shaped cane throne in the hallway was bought on hire-purchase. 'That chair is like me,' says Donna. 'It will bend; it will not break.'

*

Bridie, born in 1963, remembers little of her childhood, which frustrates her. Her mother told her to look on the bright side of the memory lapse. 'You've blacked it all out of your head,' Peggy would console her. Bridie's teenage experiences were normal. 'One night we went to a youth dance in the Creggan centre, and on the way home the IRA set a police car on fire. Then there was a shoot-out. It was great that night. We sat at the bedroom window and watched the cops flying over the fields. The helicopters were high up above us, shining searchlights down. We couldn't sleep, so when the cops and soldiers went away, we took a walk over the fields ourselves to see if we could see any of the boys.'

She took part in the riots. 'You'd see the soldiers come out of the camp behind our street and down the road towards us. So you'd run in your front door, go out into the back yard, and throw bottles over the roof into the street.' There were face-to-face confrontations. 'One time I hit a soldier with a stone. They chased after us. I was wearing a striped jumper and jeans, so I ran into the house and changed my jumper. A soldier came into the house and said to the boys: "One of you lads is after hitting us with a stone." I was shaking, maybe I wasn't, a whole patrol after me like that.' They got so used to soldiers coming through their house, at any time of day or night, with or without excuse, to arrest somebody, anybody, often without reason, that 'we used to decide among ourselves which one of us would agree to be lifted and taken off to the barracks'.

She hated school. 'I mean, I really hated it. I learned what I needed to learn, and then I didn't bother turning up if I could get away with it. Me ma always needed help anyway. But she wouldn't let us stay off school unless we cleaned the house and did the washing and cooking. She said we had to learn something.'

The education authorities finally caught up with them in 1978, and Bridie and her twin sister May ended up in the dock in Derry courthouse. Her mother did not go along that day. 'She hated courts. She was frightened of them. By the time we started appearing in them, she couldn't be bothered with them. She'd wait at home to hear the bad news.'

Margie, just married, represented the family and it was Margie who translated for Bridie and May what the Judge meant. 'I hadn't a clue what he was saying. I didn't understand. Margie was crying. She was expecting a baby. She said, "Yous are getting sent away for three years until youse are eighteen." I called the Judge a bastard.'

The twins were driven in a police car to a training school near Belfast. 'We were locked into a room. We were let out during the day to do cooking. We started crying and a Belfast girl told us to fuck up. We were only allowed to smoke five fags a day.'

After three days, they were brought to a Belfast court for the appeal. There was no one there but their lawyer. The sentence was lifted and a fine was imposed.

'Then we were brought to a barracks and we had to sit there for hours. Finally me mammy and Paddy arrived. They'd gone to the wrong court and then they'd gone to the wrong barracks. It's wild hard to find your way round Belfast.'

The government workshop which Bridie entered after she left school at sixteen was located in an abandoned Victorian school. She remembers that: 'An MP, an Englishman or somebody, came to see how we were getting on, and we voted not to allow him into the place, and the cops came with him and started shoving us about. So we stayed outside, while the Englishman went in on his own.'

She got a job in a plastics factory. This bored her. She left and signed on the dole. This bored her. She took a part-time job in a child-wear boutique, two days a week, earning six pounds a day. When a full-time job failed to materialise from the boutique, Bridie went back on the dole.

She and her new husband, Liam, squatted into a two-bedroomed flat in Creggan, which was in bad repair. Eventually they got legal tenancy of a three-bedroomed house just a few doors away from her brother Tony's house. They installed Spanish arches and brick fireplaces. Though unemployed, Liam's training in upholstery shows in the furniture re-covered in mock leather.

Their house has only been raided once, a peaceful departure from the norm that governed the lives of both before they got married. Liam's uncle, Desmond Beattie, was the second civilian ever to be killed by the army in Derry, in 1971.

*

Teenage rioting apart, neither Bridie nor Liam have been directly involved in the war. Bridie's frequent collisions with the military machine have occurred as a direct result of her family circumstances. The relationship between her and the security forces is almost strictly personal, revolving around loyalty and opposition to Paddy.

'Like, you go out for a night with the family, across the border usually, and you know you'll probably be pulled in for a search on the way home. Here come the Deerys, they say, and you know you're in for it. One night there, a wee while ago, we came in two cars to the checkpoint and they pulled in the car with Margie and Johnny in it. Then they loaded them into a jeep and set off up the road to Fort George. So we got behind the convoy, and started tooting the horn, and the soldiers tooted back. Margie and Johnny opened the back door of their jeep and waved to us. Then the Brits waved us down. So then we all got hauled into Fort George as well, me and Liam and Helen and May and June and Tony and his wife Lily. They kept us in the hall while they questioned Margie.

'They said all the Deery girls were sluts and tramps. They said Margie had quare-sized hips, that she was like a horse with the size of her teeth. May offered to take one of them out to the square for a fight. No, we weren't frightened of them. They thump us, we hit them, you get used to it.'

There are things Bridie is not used to. 'Even if there is a war going on, I don't agree with the IRA punishing young fellows for going mad. I don't agree with beating and knee-capping young fellows. When the IRA shaved Johnny's head, me ma started crying. All the young fellows get into trouble, how could they not? There's been nothing but trouble since we were born.'

Bridie doesn't take any active part in politics or attend any of the political demonstrations which occur regularly in her area. 'I don't even go on the Bloody Sunday commemorations. Me ma always warned us against taking part in marches. She was afeared something would happen to us like what happened to her.' She does go faithfully to funerals of IRA members. 'The war's over for them. They're entitled to be buried in peace, and to be noticed.'

Marriage and motherhood content her. 'The only thing that bothers me is the gambling on the poker machines; it's a waste of money and if there's one thing I hate in this life it's debt. It crippled me mammy. I've a washing machine there I'm paying for at ten pounds a week and it hangs over me. The beginning of my life I can't bear to remember, and this part I'm trying to forget.'

*

Like her twin Bridie, May also left school at sixteen only to return to a disused school for a ritual year as a government trainee. She learned metalwork and gardening and plasterwork, all of which she hugely enjoyed. 'After that, there was nothing but the shirt factory and I didn't want to go there. We'd done two weeks in the factory for work experience and I hated it, all that noise.'

She signed on the dole and spent her time rioting, or in the club for unemployed youth in Creggan. There she learned to play snooker and became a member of the Creggan United indoor seven-a-side football team, along with her younger sister Bess. The team won a Northern Ireland tournament, after playing ten matches in one day. She liked football very much, but it was not available to young women once they reached the age of twenty – May was pregnant at age twenty-one, in the same year that Bridie became pregnant. She could not face telling her mother, so she arranged that the doctor should send the letter dealing with hospital appointments to Margie's house. 'I knew Margie would open it and know what to do. I hid upstairs the day she arrived up in our house to tell me ma.' May has nothing to say about the father of her child.

A war-related injury that May sustained is the source of family jokes. She went downtown the day after a bomb went off and into her favourite pub, which had been caught in the blast. Undiscovered shards of glass, hidden in the seating, pierced her as she sat down, leaving scars in places which, her family said, would have to be revealed in order to obtain compensation. In the event, May was awarded, without contest, £500.

*

May's younger sister and football companion Bess has received no specific award or punishment since the war began. Born in 1965, Bess chose not to forsake the environs of her home and street and estate until 1987, when she signed off the dole, in absolute boredom, and got herself a job in a shirt factory across the river. The workforce is mixed. 'Some of the Protestant women are dead on. There are others you'd fight with.'

*

Tony, twin brother of Bess, grew up as bearer of his mother's messages to the world, and carrier of replies. He established his marital home a few doors from her. It was Tony who drove around town delivering her brief notes to her relatives, solicitors and priests, and Tony who usually drove her to Buncrana to play the machines. It was Tony who went to collect the death certificate for Michael. It was Tony that Peggy feared for after Michael died, as he drove around in search of those who caused his brother's death.

Tony and his childhood sweetheart Lily married when he was eighteen and she was seventeen. They lived but a few doors from each other then, and they live mid-way between their parental homes now, in Creggan Heights. Lily once got a part-time job, in a mobile shop, at a pound an hour. Tony has only ever worked on temporary youth-training schemes. They are almost unique in that they observe the strict legal guidelines laid down by the British Government for life on welfare. They do not pretend to be separated, which would enable them to claim more money as a single mother of two children and an unemployed father; neither one has ever made bogus claims about potholes; they are legal tenants of the house. They don't smoke or drink and they dislike hire-purchase. They go to Buncrana nearly every night to play the poker machines while Lily's sisters babysit and nearly every night they are pulled into the army checkpoint at the border for screening.

One night their house was raided. The police searched the kitchen and living-room, one of them showing exaggerated care as he wrapped a white handkerchief round his hand before moving objects. 'You people are fucking diseased. There are germs leaping off everything,' he said. This annoyed Lily, particularly as she had just had the sofa coverings dry-cleaned. She slapped the policeman's cheek.

*

Tony's younger brother Martin, has also come through the war remarkably unscathed. 'I'm the law-abiding citizen in this family,' he is inclined to joke, though he dodged many schooldays and hid in the coalshed at the end of the back-garden. His sisters used to bring him tea and sandwiches there, unknown to Peggy. 'Sometimes I'd sneak up to the window and just look in at me mammy, but she never copped on.'

Sometimes Martin is hauled into the police barracks or an army fort for hours at a time, because newly arriving soldiers mistake him for one of his brothers, or because he gets caught in a family squabble at checkpoints, but he has not been in jail. Nor does he wish to go there. Martin is under no illusion about the horror of that.

He married a woman from the same Donegal village as Necky's fiancée. He walked across the border to his wedding, in 1987, taking an officially closed border road out of Creggan. He and his brother Johnny strolled over the hills in their rented tuxedos, in order to avoid any possible clash with the police or the army. The Deery wedding convoys had been searched in the past. They got to the church on time.

Martin and his wife Patricia then squatted into the Creggan house which a relative left after finding a better squat.

*

June, born in 1967, is an adamant young mother of few words. She did not enjoy her wedding day, she says, she did not like the two days spent in England while her husband Michael looked for a job there, she didn't like their mobile home in Donegal, and she liked going back with her baby to live with Peggy within the year.

*

On the day Peggy's last and fourteenth child was born, 18 May 1971, the local Catholic bishop issued a prescription for the future of infants such as Bernadette Devlin Deery. He expressed worry about the civil disorder which was beginning to convulse the North: parents, said Neil Farren, should sacrifice their leisure hours and spend more time at home with their children, to keep them off the streets. The *Derry Journal* published an editorial that day, warning that the demand for contraceptive facilities in Ireland presaged a pagan future and a falling away from Christian standards of decency. In the first year of her life Bernadette's father died and her mother was shot. She wrote a letter to her mother from New York where she was sent at the age of twelve on a holiday for disadvantaged Derry children. It said:

Dear mammy,
The family I'm staying with never bought me nothing, so tell everybody not to be expecting a gift. Mammy, I never got a letter from you and I am very worried. What did you not write for? I've been writing to you very often. Every day I run down to the mail box to see if I've got any mail but I still love you.
Bernadette.

Married to the IRA

Helen and Margie carrying their brother Paddy's coffin

Paddy's young and pregnant wife Colette insisted that he get a job. Within eight weeks of his wedding in July 1976, Paddy was on the night shift at an industrial plant outside of town. Colette had been working since she left school at sixteen. Before she settled down to motherhood at nineteen years of age she went through a series of jobs, first in a shirt factory, then on the assembly line, then in an electronics plant.

The expenses of the wedding were cobbled together out of a loan Paddy got from a bank in the expectation of government compensation for his eye and a loan Colette got from the Credit Union. The honeymoon was spent in Dublin, where Peggy had once treated them, while they were courting, to a New Year's Eve weekend in a posh hotel. 'You should enjoy yourselves while you're young,' she had insisted. She paid for the trip out of her own Bloody Sunday compensation and came along as chaperone, bringing as her escort her dead husband's brother, Buddy. Buddy and Paddy shared one room and Peggy and Colette shared another. 'There was a bedside phone for room service,' Colette remembers, 'and Peggy was delighted with the luxury of that. She phoned reception and ordered drinks in a swanky voice. Then we all had Pernod and Smithwicks. Paddy mocked his mammy for keeping me in a room separate from him. He placed his glass eye on the floor under me and said "Sure I can already see up her clothes."'

Then he went on the run in Donegal.

Colette used to travel over to meet him at dances. 'If I wasn't there on the first bus, he'd go into a jealous rage. Then if he couldn't get hitting anybody at the dance, he'd try and pick a fight with the guards [the Irish police].'

One afternoon in Derry the bus in which she travelled was stopped at an IRA checkpoint. This regular show of defiance was meant to challenge army supremacy in the area. Colette looked out the window and recognised Paddy.

The newlyweds moved into the home of Colette's parents to await the birth of the first baby. Paddy was not at ease there. 'Our house was too quiet for him. There was only my mammy and daddy and me and him. He missed the noise up in Peggy's place, with people coming and going all the time. Even his eating habits were different. He couldn't get used to what my daddy made for dinner. Paddy liked greasy stuff, fried food, not boiled potatoes and cabbage.' The years of eating fast-food on the run, quickly prepared in homes where he sought shelter, had left their mark.

The normal routine of family life was difficult for him, especially in a family which had had enough of the war.

Colette's mother and father wanted no part of it, after their experiences of 1972. 'There was a wild lot of people killed that year, and then there was Operation Motorman. My brother was out that night, and he got shot for building a barricade. I mind that night. The jeeps were as big as houses. They wanted to take him across the border to Letterkenny Hospital, but my father said that he had nothing to hide. He had his rights, he said. My father used to be a stoker in the Royal Navy, in Singapore. He was a Protestant before he married my mother. I mind ye could have stuck two or three fingers into the hole in my brother's head where the bullet hit him. My mammy was on valium for years and years after that. One day my father told her she'd have to come off them, because she hadn't been out of the house in years. She had terrible withdrawal symptoms. She still doesn't like coming outside. We've another brother who went away in the middle of it, over to England and we don't know where he is.'

The marriage faltered and Paddy returned to his mother's house. One night he came back drunk, and broke a window trying to gain access to Colette. 'I cleaned up the glass before my parents came in. I didn't want my father to know. He always said I was too good even for the Prince of Wales.'

*

A reconciliation was effected before the birth of the child. Paddy came to her, excited and proud, to announce that he had found a home for them. He and his mother had been scanning the paper every day, looking at the death columns. An old, single man had died and Peggy and Paddy went down to see his relatives. They gave them the keys to the old man's bedsitter in the high-rise building around which the Bloody Sunday victims had been shot and Paddy squatted in after the old man's funeral.

The five-storey sub-standard structure, built in 1965 and pulled down in 1987, was known as Alcatraz, but to Paddy and Colette the bedsitter was 'a palace. We were made legal tenants at once. Nobody else wanted to live there. It was great until it hit us what we had done. We were up on the fifth floor, trapped with a baby. The room had a double bed and a cot, a wardrobe and a dressing table, a coffee-table and a suite of furniture squeezed in.' The couple were locked together, for long periods of the day and night, in their room far above the ground because Paddy had been forced to quit his job. 'He used to come home with his good eye nearly closed, and a big stye on it that never went away. He had to come out on the sick and go on permanent invalidity.'

Colette visited her parents every day in Creggan. Every time she went to Creggan she pushed the baby in its pram over to the offices of a housing co-operative. The private enterprise initiative had been started by Fr Anthony Mulvey in a desperate attempt to meet the clamour for housing.' I had the man in that office tortured. After only four months, he finally agreed to give me a place. First we had a two-bedroomed flat, then a three-bedroomed house where I've lived ever since. I love it.'

While Colette made a home, Paddy fought a sporadic war. They would quarrel about this, he would attempt to settle down, and then he would be off soldiering again. 'One night he came home and he'd been drinking, but he wasn't paralatic. He could talk. He took a drink so he could face me with his news. He started to cry and he said, "Colette, I miss the IRA." He said he could never live without it; he had to be in it; he said it was the only thing made sense with a war going on. He said, "It's part of my life." I said, "I'm part of your life. The wains are part of your life. I was content with my life with you and the wains." He knew the way I took it, he knew I took this hard, but he said he felt all the way inside himself that he had to be part of the IRA.'

Paddy had one other passion in his life, for which he was famed. He adored cars. The white Avenger which his mother bought him was followed by a blue Cortina before marriage, then a second-hand green Audi, then an orange hatch-back Datsun, all funded by Peggy in an effort to get him out of the IRA. As Peggy's funds declined, so did the state of the cars, and the Datsun, an old banger, was purchased for £200. 'He cried the night his brother crashed the Cortina. The tears rolled out of his one eye, when he went down and saw the way the door had caved in.' If he had nothing else to do, his life-long friend and IRA companion said of him, Paddy liked nothing better than to go for a run in the car. 'Any car. He would say: "Let's hijack a car and drive it round Donegal." This might be in the middle of the night. The car was Paddy's real home.'

As an IRA volunteer, he spent less and less time in the home Colette established.

*

When the £20,000 compensation for his eye came through in 1981, Paddy and Colette had a rough lesson in banking. To the amount he had been borrowing in advance since 1976 was added interest, so that only £9,000 remained of the anticipated fortune. Paddy bought a sitting-room suite for his mother, gave her a gift of £1,000 and then bought a modest old house in a settled part of the Bogside hoping to renovate and resell at a profit with the help of generous British government grants for refurbishment. He also bought a laundry van. 'It only lasted a couple of months. He was making £200 a week delivering the washing then he gave the keys to his brothers, and went back to the IRA. One day he stuck a gun under the laundry, and there was a shoot-out with the army and that was the end of the van.'

Efforts to combine membership of the IRA with a working life failed hopelessly, as Paddy was continually forced to go on the run, but he did have one spectacular entrepreneurial success with his comrade-in-arms, who recalled their great Christmas coup: 'Moving round houses on the run you get a feel for the market, for what the children want for Christmas. So we bought a whole lot of toys, and arranged house-parties. You'd leave the toys in somebody's house, and people would come and choose. We had no overheads, so we undercut all the traders in town. We made a packet that year, but it was only seasonal. If we'd wanted to keep going in business all year round we'd have had to give up the war. But at least we learned better what we were fighting for. There's an immoral amount of profit in big business.'

Any hopes Colette might have entertained for a settled family life as Paddy grew older faded in 1982 when the supergrass system erupted and Paddy was named by both the Derry informers. Paddy was not at home when the police came looking for him. Alerted by the mass round-up of suspects he had stayed across the border in Buncrana, the seaside resort on the Donegal coast which has seen better days. He was there for five years and he lived, says Colette, like a bachelor. The enforced rest and recreation from active service, in a hostile environment, was a recipe for disaster. Paddy drank a lot, and when he was persuaded to give up excessive drinking, he became a poker-machine addict, spending endless days in cheap arcades, seeking the hypnotic comfort of life by numbers. 'You could walk in and if he was playing the one-armed bandits he wouldn't even notice you were there.'

Colette went down to Buncrana on the bingo-bus, two nights during the week, to see him, leaving babysitting arrangements in the hands of the multiple Deery in-laws. From Friday to Sunday she stayed with him in Buncrana, bringing the children with her. On Monday, on return to Derry, she bought groceries and cigarettes which she sent down on the bingo bus or with Peggy who was crossing the border daily to visit Paddy, or Pio or Helen or Johnny.

The single man's allowance which Paddy received on the Irish dole barely paid the rent of the various flats he took in Buncrana. Colette subsidised him to the point where, she says, 'I was living on nothing.' Paddy sold the house he had bought, receiving in exchange a sum of money and a mobile home. Colette and the children joined him for the summer in the mobile, which he had parked near a Penal mass-rock on a beautiful stretch of beach and sanddunes on the out-skirts of Buncrana. Other IRA families shared the summer beach with them. 'One day, when Paddy was up gambling on the machines, I had the place gleaming, the clothes washed and dried and the dinner on. I went to the mobile next door for a smoke, when the next thing I noticed was black clouds coming in my direction. My mobile was in flames. The whole thing burnt down. I lost my money, my welfare books, my handbag and most of the clothes.'

Paddy then rented a flat in Buncrana and invited Colette down for the weekend. 'It was a beautiful big bungalow, with two big stone peacocks in the driveway. Paddy led me through the garden and out the back and to a wee shed where he was living.'

*

In March 1983, two things happened. The health board in Derry ordered Paddy to attend a medical examination to prove that he still qualified for invalidity pension. He did not dare come across the border and was struck off the pension scheme. Colette thought it was the end of the world. 'While he was on it, the rent was paid and the children qualified for free school dinners.' She moved onto the welfare rolls as a single parent. The second thing that happened was that Colette went to Buncrana on St Patrick's night, 17 March, to attend a dance celebrating the Republic's patron saint. In an expansive mood, she and Paddy decided that she should not return home to Derry with the other revellers, but that they should book into a bed-and-breakfast hotel. It was on that night, she thinks, that her last child was conceived.

The baby was born on 14 December, and Paddy slipped into Derry to visit his family. 'We had two good weeks, Christmas and New Year's, and then on 2 January, when we were lying in bed, about four in the morning, I heard a knock at the door. You'd know the police knock anywhere. It shattered a pane of glass. I said to Paddy: "What the fuck are you going to do?" but he wasn't right wakened. He scrambled out of our bed and ran into the children's room and hid under a bed, against the wall. His foot stuck out of the bottom of the bed and I pushed it in, and then I went to the kitchen. The police were there. They said, "Is Patrick here?" and I said, "What the fuck are you on about, I haven't seen him in years." The baby was sitting there, only three weeks old, so I'd made myself out to be a right hooker, but that's the kind of thing they believe about us anyway.'

The police moved into her bedroom, where one of them felt the sheets and said that both sides of the double bed were warm. 'That's because I'm hot stuff,' said Colette. At this point she felt she had nothing to lose, since all was obviously lost anyway: Paddy had left his socks and shoes on the floor. One policeman looked at these items. He asked her who owned the shoes and socks. 'Them's mine,' she said. 'Fuck, mister, this house is freezing and I wear them into bed, shoes, socks, the lot, it doesn't mean anything to me if they fit or not.' The policeman looked at her again and accompanied her into the second bedroom where the two other children lay awake. 'Young Patrick winked at me to show he knew the score. He was only eight. I could feel his father breathing under the bed that was against the wall. I bit my lip and I could feel the blood dripping. The policeman looked at me and I thought he was going to beat the face off me for being a liar. Then he went out and said there was nobody in there but the wains and me. I think he felt sorry for me. Maybe he just had a heart. It's hard to believe the police have hearts, but that one did.'

After the police left, Paddy decided to make his escape. The house faced onto a road on the other side of which were open fields leading to the border. While they whispered together, Colette noticed a man's shadow through the window pane. 'You learn to notice all that kind of stuff. You get into these things when you're married to a boy like mine.' Paddy argued that the seconds which would elapse between soldiers shouting 'Halt' and then opening fire would give him sufficient time to get across the road and over the hedge. 'It was ridiculous. The Brits were all over the place outside, and I was giving him a sermon inside about his big head, him and his notions about how fast he could run.'

The matter was settled when an army helicopter arrived and hovered overhead, lighting the field and road up like a stage. The soldiers fanned out to search the area. Paddy and Colette spent the night clutching each other under the bed-clothes. Next day he returned to Buncrana. Soon after, the welfare authorities arrived to ask Colette to account for the baby born to a single parent. They said she need not name the father if it was embarrassing. 'I told them it was Paddy's child. I said he sometimes came up to visit his wains, and he stayed over one night, and that even if I loved him I couldn't live with him. They said that was all right.'

*

Colette had in any case come to the conclusion that she was truly a single parent. Increasingly, when she made baby-sitting arrangements so that she could go and see Paddy in Buncrana, she received last minute phone calls cancelling the arrangement. 'He never had the nerve to phone me direct. He would call one of his sisters and leave word for me not to come down that night, because he had to go away somewhere. There was one Easter in particular, the sun was splitting the stones and the other women went down to see their men, and I was left sitting in Creggan. So his sister Bridie eventually said to me that this was happening too often. She said I should go out on my own anyhow and enjoy myself. But I was that used to staying in by then that I didn't want to go out. I didn't know how to. I went and talked to Peggy about what Paddy was doing and she said, "That's not right." I was wild about Peggy, you could tell her anything, talk about your marriage. We spent four hours talking about it, just me and her. She said she would straighten him out, but sure she couldn't, the IRA was in him and that kind of life.'

Colette started going out then, in Derry. Bingo was boring for her, so she went to the musical pubs, especially the ones frequented by the IRA. 'For all I gave out about it, the IRA life was mine too. At least they understood how things were for me.' The minute she heard music she hit the dance floor. 'I just loved it. I still do. I love dancing.' Paddy tried to stop her going out. Sometimes he would send for her, and tell her when she went to meet him in Buncrana that it was all right for a married man to go out on his own, but that: 'It didn't look right in a married woman. He said people would think there was something wrong with the marriage if they saw a married woman out without her husband.' He was also jealous. These Buncrana reconciliations did not work. Paddy invariably reverted back to the lifestyle of a drinking, driving, bachelor boy in the house which he now shared with fifteen men on the run. Colette obtained a legal separation.

*

One night a few months after Necky was killed, Paddy went with his brother-in-law Seamus to a cabaret pub in Donegal where the British tabloid page-three starlet Linda Lusardi was making a personal appearance. On the way home, the car which Paddy was driving was stopped at a garda checkpoint. Paddy was afraid of being charged again with drunken driving, having already spent three months in jail in the South. As the breathalyser was produced, Paddy jumped back in the van and drove a short distance in the dark. He stopped just in front of the British border post, got out and stood there, drunk. The guards arrived alongside him, bringing Seamus with them. Within seconds, Paddy and Seamus found themselves on the Northern side, in the custody of the RUC.

Paddy then spent six months in Crumlin Jail, in Belfast, on foot of the supergrass charges. Colette went to see him every Tuesday, bringing the three children on the long journey. She cried after her first visit. 'I'd never been in prison before. It was creepy. At the start, I was grand, smiling away, but Paddy could tell the way I took it. He was the best of crack, keeping things going during the visits, cheering everybody up. He told me to listen to "Lady in Red", a smoochy song that was at the top of the hit parade. He said that that was about us.' While Colette played 'Lady in Red' at home, thinking of Paddy in prison, the son of the queen of England, Prince Andrew, on his honeymoon cruise on the royal yacht *Britannia*, had staff play the same record while he danced on deck with his wife.

Paddy wrote optimistic letters home. The supergrass trials involving him having already collapsed, he was confident that the authorities would not stage another trial, especially for him. It would mean bringing Robert Quigley and Raymond Gilmour back from South Africa or Cyprus or wherever the British Government had fixed them up with a completely new identity. Besides which, the Anglo-Irish Agreement, promising closer security co-operation between the British and Irish Governments, had just been signed, and it was an unwritten part of that agreement that the British would adhere to proper legal procedures in court. The most encouraging sign for Paddy was that his sister Pio, who had failed to turn up for her supergrass trial, was living freely in Derry. Paddy regarded his detention as a temporary internment and looked forward to confirmation in court that the charges would be dropped. The list of accusations against him was as long as his arm, Colette said. She took the same delicate view of these charges that others did who knew him well. 'Paddy done a lot in his day but he didn't do what the supergrass said he did. The charges were all wrong.'

On the eve of his thirty-first birthday, in November 1986, Paddy wrote to his mother about his forthcoming appearance in court. The letter was officially stamped 'Number 2260. Paddy Deery. Her Majesty's Prison, Belfast. Censored'.

Hello Mum,
Well mam, how's things going with you? Alls well I hope. Martin and May were up here today (Thursday), they were telling me that you phoned the solicitor about the tenth. Well, I hope so (Ha Ha) so you never know I might be seeing yous all very soon, like the 11th maybe. (Ha Ha). A very happy birthday it would be. (Ha Ha). 31 on Thursday. I was glad to hear you got sorted out with the attendance allowance (magic) and I hope you're not spending it too foolish. Well now I will finish off for now and you never know I might see yous all on Monday or Tuesday. Until I see you, very soon I hope,
All my love,
Your son,
Paddy. xxxxx

He did see them on his birthday, and he told Colette he was

going to settle down. He said he was getting too old for life on the run. He suggested that if they started going out together they would get on better. If he went out on his own, he said, he would drink and fight. Paddy went to his IRA commander and expressed his doubts about his ability to carry on. For all his bravado, he had never had the steady nerve required for direct armed confrontation, and he had developed feelings of inadequacy about being only a getaway driver. He went through the withdrawal symptoms common to many IRA men who felt that retirement from the war, and concentration on family, was tantamount to loss of manhood. He felt ashamed. In the seventies, the IRA now admits, such retirement from the fray was commonly greeted with jeers. As the war lengthened and young men became family men, they began to treat each other with more sensitivity. Paddy started concentrating on his family in 1987.

*

Then he started going out again on his own. Exasperated, Colette said to him: 'If you want me to keep you in this family, go out and get a job.' Paddy got a seven-month stint labouring in Creggan, helping to build a health centre. Colette knew that he kept to himself the twenty-pound bonus paid every Friday night, but she said nothing because Paddy smoked sixty cigarettes a day to keep himself occupied. 'The police and army had him tortured. They made him angry all the time. We'd take the children across the border to a leisure centre on a Sunday afternoon and they used to lean in the car and call him one-eye. I think that's terrible. All the rows I ever had with him I never called him that. They were driving him back to square one. They'd hold a hand grenade in the window, or threaten to shoot him some night. They'd haul us in to Fort George and hold us there for four hours at a time, wains and all. Paddy was distracted. He'd always been bitter, but they made him more bitter. He'd start saying this was no life for his wains to face, that the war would have to go on until the Brits had left, for he wouldn't want the wains to lead the life he'd led. Then he went to Sinn Féin and asked how come every other child had got away on holidays for the deprived and his hadn't. So young Patrick suddenly found himself on a trip the Americans paid for, I think it was Noraid. He ended up spending two months in Alaska. Can you picture it, Alaska, sure Buncrana was better.'

In August 1987 Paddy was lifted and brought to Castlereagh for seven days' interrogation. In October the labouring job ended. On 28 October Paddy volunteered as getaway driver on an IRA bombing mission. The plan was to pack the steering wheel of a stolen car with explosives, drive it downtown, plant a small bomb, abandon the stolen car and effect a getaway in a second car. The police would take possession of the abandoned car, and drive a literally ticking time-bomb into the police station to check for fingerprint evidence.

A member of the IRA was later to tell Colette that it was his job to drive the car that was packed with explosives. Paddy, the driving expert, was to be in charge of the getaway car. The team assembled in the playground of a small Irish-language school, tucked away in the Creggan housing estate, about two hundred yards from Peggy Deery's house. At the last minute, around twenty past one, this man says, Paddy insisted on swopping jobs. Paddy got behind the steering wheel of the lethal vehicle. Eddie McSheffrey sat in the passenger seat with the bomb in his lap. The bomb exploded. Eddie McSheffrey died instantly. Paddy lived long enough to be cradled in the lap of his brother Tony, who had been driving home for dinner in Peggy's motability car when a crowd stopped him.

*

Colette was in her own home, with her father, when she heard the explosion. Her father had been showing her a letter he had received from England and they were discussing what to do about the contents. The letter concerned her missing brother whom her father had been trying to trace. 'Bridie came over to tell me. She said Paddy was on his way to the hospital. I felt just drained. When I got to Peggy's they'd heard he was dead. They gave me a valium. It confused my head. The doctor came and offered to write me a prescription for anti-depressants. I said I wasn't taking any more. I want to live without tablets, not get hooked on them, bottle after bottle. My daddy said to take them just for a week, but I said no, look what had happened to my mammy. Daddy didn't know when he said it that it would take the full week just to get Paddy buried, with the police and Sinn Féin and the bishop fighting over it.'

Colette dreams about it all. 'Sometimes I jump up in the middle of the night. I see Paddy sitting in the car. I think of the bomb going off. It plays on your mind. It's hard to accept he's dead, when all I saw of him dead was a photo on top of his coffin. They wouldn't let me open it.' She has a tape recording which she sometimes plays of a night she and Paddy spent at home together when he got out of prison. 'We'd been dancing and carrying on. You can hear us talking through the music, "Lady in Red", and Johnny Logan singing "What's Another Year?".'

One week after Paddy was buried, on Poppy Day, a Poppy Day such as the one on which he was born, the IRA left a bomb near the war memorial in Enniskillen in County Fermanagh. It exploded without warning, slaughtering eleven of the Protestants who had gathered there for Remembrance Sunday. Colette started getting anonymous letters through the post, showing the faces of those Protestants who had lived and were maimed. 'I hated bombs anyway. They could hurt a whole lot of people. I don't think it's right for anybody to die like that, Paddy or the Protestants or anybody, to be blown to smithereens. What's it all for? Paddy used to say the fight wasn't against Protestants. He went to my grandfather's wake, and he was a Protestant, and Paddy sat in there with the Protestants, laughing away and cracking jokes. He was always joking, always full of laughs. I think that's what I liked best about Paddy. He made me laugh. When something was wild bad, Paddy would lift your spirits up all the time.'

After Paddy's death, Colette visited Peggy, bringing her

children, every Friday and Saturday night. 'The two of us were feeling wild sorry for one another. She told me to get myself out and about, even once a week. "Nobody expects you to sit around for the rest of your life," she said. I said to her she should go out too. Maybe someday, she said, but she wanted to stay in bed and see if she could dream about Paddy and Necky, the way everybody else was doing. That was killing her, everybody dreaming about them except her.'

Colette has noticed the change which this severing of the links has brought to her home. 'Like, I used to change the furniture around the house every single day, maybe every hour. Paddy used to remark on it. He said he didn't know where he'd be sitting from one visit to the next. Now the furniture stays in the one place all the time. The wains' nerves are settling down. The people up here treat them just like any other children. They never really knew Paddy anyway, it was always just Colette and her wains. The wains don't jump up any more the way they used to if Paddy was around and the army came by on patrol. "There's a jeep, Daddy," they'd say. I've explained to them that the army and the police can't do us any harm. They can do us no more harm now.'

In May 1988, the welfare authorities requested Colette to attend an interview to discuss her position. They told her that three letters had been sent to Paddy since June 1986, asking him to come before an interview board to discuss his permanent invalidity pension. They asked Colette if she could inform them of his whereabouts. Colette told them several things, succinctly. Paddy had lost his disability pension in 1983. He had been unable to respond to their letters in 1986 since he was in jail. She had applied for a death grant to bury him in October 1987, and they had kindly awarded it. He was now dead and in the cemetery. 'Incoming army regiments, please note.'

I Absolve You . . .

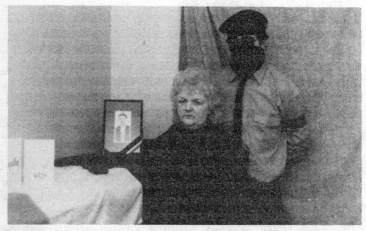

Peggy and the IRA Guard of Honour at Paddy's coffin

During the six days it took to bury Paddy Deery and Eddie McSheffrey, Derry was communally sundered as priest, politician and policeman engaged in debate about the burial process. The corpses were kept encoffined in their homes, under an IRA guard-of-honour while the protagonists argued. They came to no agreement. 'That was the worst time of my life, after Bloody Sunday,' says Bishop Edward Daly, for whom the funerals had become a resignation issue. In the North, now, the dead are symbols through which party politicians, paramilitaries, Church and State mediate their respective and irreconcilable philosophies.

There had been a brief while in Derry when funerals were not a source of political contention. Death, then, was so rare as to be awe-inspiring, irrespective of the tribal colouring of the victim. The obsequies of any stranger, killed locally and buried however far away, merited respectful and full coverage.

Lance-corporal William Joliffe, of the Royal Military Police, was the first British soldier to die in Derry, on 3 March 1971. The *Derry Journal* informed its readers that he was eighteen years old and came from Chippenham in England, where he was buried with full military honours. His coffin was draped in a Union Jack, and a wreath from his widowed mother was placed on top of the flag, along with his red military police cap, red armband and white belt. The coffin was laid on a Howitzer gun-carriage, which was towed by an army Land-Rover. Four military policemen on chestnut horses led a cortege of thirty cars to the cemetery, where a thirteen-man firing party fired three rounds and trumpets played the Last Salute.

Five months later, the first IRA volunteer was shot dead in Derry, on 18 August 1971. The tricolour-draped coffin of Eamonn Lafferty, aged nineteen, a baker by trade, was brought to the cathedral where requiem mass was said by his cousin, a missionary priest. Fourteen priests and the then bishop of Derry, Neil Farren, were present in the church. A guard-of-honour of six men, wearing distinctive Republican berets, escorted the coffin out of church and led priests and mourners to the cemetery, where a declared member of the Belfast Provisional IRA gave an oration for the 'brave soldier of Ireland'. The Westminster member of Parliament for Derry, John Hume, personally asked British soldiers to leave the street in which they had taken up position so that the mourners might return home in peace, without their provocative presence.

No volley of shots was fired at the graveside of Eamonn Lafferty. There was neither need nor desire to mark him as a man apart. Attendance at the mass and funeral had shown that he was seen as less a soldier than a defender and respected member of his community. *The Irish Times*, in an editorial written before his death, had said of the IRA that 'one can believe their intentions are not sectarian'.

The mournful innocence of those days had been buried under a welter of death and destruction by the time Paddy Deery blew himself up. His death, and that of Eddie McSheffrey, brought close to three thousand the number of paramilitaries, soldiers, policemen and civilians who have died by bomb, bullet and assassination in Northern Ireland. Hundreds of others have died as the war overspilled into the Republic, Great Britain and the rest of Europe.

*

Bishop Edward Daly knew, better than most, the implications of the proposed burial rites of these two IRA volunteers. He had come of political age on Bloody Sunday. It seared him. Like others who survived, he is wont to refer back to it in any political discussion about the North. He has never since regarded the British Army as a neutral power.

His relationship with the British Army had been rather more trusting before Bloody Sunday. On one occasion, he and a local politician had defused an abandoned IRA bomb when the army refused to go near it. The army was afraid of ambush by the IRA; the IRA was afraid of ambush by the army. Both sides placed their trust in Fr Edward Daly and Ivan Cooper. After consulting an army bomb-disposal expert by telephone, the priest and the politician disconnected the wires designed to detonate sixteen pounds of plastic explosive.

On Bloody Sunday, that army shot at this fleeing priest. A bullet killed the teenager who ran alongside him. The teenager was laughing as he died. Jack Duddy had never thought to find himself running with his pastor. The televised image of Father Daly, carrying the boy's body, ducking the bullets and waving a white handkerchief as he turned to face the army, was flashed around the world. Recalling the moment, he said with endearing honesty that he understood why any young person might want to join the IRA. When he was subsequently made bishop of Derry, parishioners strewed flower petals in his path.

Peggy Deery was among the people anointed where they lay on the streets on Bloody Sunday, by Fr Daly and other priests. The awesome last rites of the Church to which they cleaved dignified them, honoured them, exalted them, wherever they were found, in whatever condition they were found, bleeding and frightened, dying and dead, on the barricades, in courtyards, in kitchens, in alleyways, on waste ground, in the Bogside. In the name of their God, in the presence of the British Army, their priests blessed them, forgave them their sins, and commended them to the mercy of their God:

> Through this holy anointing, may the Lord in His love and mercy help you with the grace of the Holy Spirit, amen. May the Lord who frees you from your sin, save you and raise you up, amen. I absolve you from all the sins of your whole life, in the name of the Father, Son and Holy Spirit, amen.

Those same words were said in 1987, fifteen years later, over Peggy's son as he lay speechless, conscious, and dying, amid the wreckage of his own bomb, near the Catholic church in Creggan estate. A priest in a purple silk stole traced the sign of the cross with sacramental oil upon the head and hands of Paddy Deery. Prayers of commendation to God's mercy were said for the already departed soul of Eddie McSheffrey.

The priest was confident that his actions had the full support of his bishop, though Edward Daly had publicly declared that members of the IRA subjected themselves to automatic excommunication from the Catholic Church. 'They are not freedom fighters. They are not engaged in a struggle for freedom. They are engaged in a ruthless and unprincipled campaign for power through murder, terror and intimidation. They act directly in face of the commandment, Thou shalt not kill. They do not deserve support, shelter or protection from any true follower of Jesus Christ.'

Nevertheless, as Bishop Daly confirms, no priest, bishop or pope could know or judge the state of mind and conscience of a person in the last moments of life. In theory, in practise and in theology it is assumed that there is always time before death for repentance. The priest who anointed, and did not judge, *in extremis*, the two men lying on blasted ground, assumed that he was ministering to Catholics. They were not strangers. He knew them both. 'I knew they would have wanted it that way,' he says.

*

Bishop Edward Daly did not quarrel with the assumption that his parishioners had died in the full embrace of the Catholic Church. His expressed concern was for the political status that some sought to accord Paddy Deery and Eddie McSheffrey, after death, under the aegis and within the precincts of the Church. Requiem mass for the repose of the souls of both of these dead men would be offered in the presence of their relatives and friends, he announced, but the bodily remains of these paramilitaries would not be allowed into any church in his diocese.

The funerals were postponed, while the families laid beseeching siege to him to honour the Catholic dead in body and soul. The plight in which the people and their prelate were trapped is etched bleakly in his speech. 'I did not sleep for four nights. To care for the dead, to comfort people who mourn, my whole life is centred round that. I am a parish priest. For the first time in my life I said no to people with perfectly valid demands, to Nora McGilloway, to Peggy Deery ...'

The police too, had their demands. They wanted no para-military funerals in the streets of Derry. They wanted a civilian ceremonial which would conform in the public domain to British norms of law and order. The police were determined to enforce their norms.

The IRA had their demand also. They wanted a para-military tribute, confirmed by centuries of Irish tradition, to their dead volunteers. They wanted to fire a volley of shots over the coffins. The political wing of the IRA, Sinn Féin, was fully in accord with this demand. The families of the two dead men allowed the IRA to stand guard over the bodies, in their homes, while protracted negotiations began.

Derry was suffused with dread. The scenes which had marked the funeral of IRA volunteer Gerard Logue, some months before, left little doubt as to the outcome of this one. It had taken twelve hours to bring Gerard Logue's corpse from his home to the cemetery via the chapel, and the short route had been marked by hand-to-hand fighting, as Republicans and police fought for control. The cortege was accompanied by four hundred policemen, eighty armoured Land-Rovers, two helicopters, and one thousand mourners. Four drummers leading the procession competed with Protestant bystanders who blew horns and threw stones. The respite that might have been expected when the coffin was brought into the sanctuary of the grounds of a Catholic church was shattered when the IRA appeared in the porch of the church and fired a volley of shots. The priest was aghast. The mourners cheered. The police, honouring sanctuary, were humiliated.

Bishop Edward Daly was affronted and shaken to the core. The precincts of the church had been desecrated. The authority of the Church, vested in him, had been dismissed by those whom he had deemed excommunicated from that Church. His parishioners had applauded these people. 'And it was a premeditated, planned act. The guns had been stashed in the confessional. They put on their hoods in the confessional. The central issue was a breach of trust.'

He issued an immediate edict. The remains of para-militaries would no longer be allowed into any Catholic church in Derry. His episcopal anger was tinged with remembrance. 'However noble their original intentions may have been', said the bishop who had come through Bloody Sunday. The IRA succumbed at once, with a solemn guarantee that it would never again fire shots in chapels or their precincts. The *Derry Journal* covered its retreat with a face-saving volley aimed at the size and nature of the police presence at funerals. 'It is intimidating, and intended to be so.'

Before the communal wounds had healed, they were re-opened by the deaths of Paddy Deery and Eddie

McSheffrey. While the bishop stuck unhappily by his edict, the RUC pressed home their advantage, surrounding the homes of the dead men, issuing their own edicts as to how these funerals would be conducted, seeking reassurances from the families that there would be no paramilitary display on the streets; no volley of shots; no beret, gloves or belt laid on top of the coffins.

'I felt proud, dead proud, felt real joy, felt happy,' said Johnny Deery of the sight of his brother Paddy's tricolour-draped coffin being brought home from the hospital. His eight sisters, who took turns to carry the coffin through the streets, felt 'too proud to cry', said Margie. The RUC did not object to the tricolour. The tension felt in Derry was not in any case about the outcome of the projected battle between the RUC and the IRA. By now, mourners expected to suffer on the way to the cemetery. The tension was about the outcome of the battle for authority between Bishop Edward Daly and the Republicans.

The Republicans repeated their word of honour that the funeral, within church precincts, would proceed strictly according to his criteria. The families trusted the word of the Republicans as fervently as they trusted the word of the bishop. The bishop repeated his distrust of Republicans.

*

Peggy Deery trusted her cooking pot. She made mince stew. She sat Paddy's wife Colette down in the kitchen to eat this stew. 'She knew I hadn't been eating. She made a big pot of stew, and she put me there in that chair and she said, "Eat." She put the food in my mouth. She made me eat it.'

While Colette ate in the kitchen, a steady stream of people came through the front door and into the bedroom where masked men, arms folded behind their backs, legs akimbo, stood stern guard over the closed coffin in which her dead husband was sealed. The people knelt and prayed, discussed the bishop, and went outside again to run the gauntlet of police and soldiers.

'The house was a like a dancehall. You had to squeeze in between the people. My sisters made sandwiches for them, and women I hadn't seen for years, girls I'd been to school with, they made tea. After Peggy made me eat in the kitchen she said to me: "Now you're going into the bath." But the bath was full of wreaths, wilting in the water after all them days. So Bess put my head into the basin, and washed my hair, and then she tonged my hair and blow-dried it, and then she did that with all the Deery women, washing and drying and blow-drying, and then Peggy inspected us and she said, "Now," she said, "now yous all look like Christians".'

However they looked, they scarcely knew what they were doing, said Colette. 'There were reporters here at twenty to nine in the morning, asking us what decision we'd made. There were priests coming morning, noon and night, bringing letters from the bishop. There were other priests, saying they'd say a mass outside the gates of the cathedral if the bishop wouldn't let us in. There was a rat, with its head cut off, shoved through the letterbox in the middle of the night. There were policemen and soldiers outside the house, all night, all day, all that week.'

There was disbelief, confusion and dismay that their bishop would not trust them to distinguish the difference between obeisance to God and resistance to the police. Many Republican homes in Derry give pride of place to photographs of Edward Daly, in the company of Republican parents and children on Confirmation Day, when the children are received into the Catholic Church as 'soldiers of Christ'. The bishop, on a tranquil day, is bitter-sweet about this. 'Sure some Republicans are holier than the rest of us.'

The days before the burial of Paddy Deery and Eddie McSheffrey were not tranquil. 'If I had given in, and allowed the remains into church, and there had been a fight in church grounds with the police, and people had been injured, or killed, where would that have left me? I might as well have packed up and gone away.' His apprehension was well grounded. The Republicans, thinking through the scenario, were pondering a similar outcome.

Their public analysis in the names of the families, though couched in the most contrite, soft and beguiling terms, absolved them in advance of any responsibility for the outcome by linking the actions of the bishop, no matter what he did, with those of the RUC:

> Given that (IRA) guarantee, we would hope that the Bishop would allow us to bury our loved ones in peace, and with dignity. This is our deepest wish and we hope that Bishop Daly, as a caring and humane man, will recognize how important it is to us at this most tragic time. We would also hope that the RUC and Bishop Daly would respect our grieving families and leave us in peace.

Peace, as was well known to the bishop, the RUC and the IRA, meant peace to fire a live volley, during a funeral, in tribute to dead members of the IRA.

The priests of Derry were caught up in the drama. Paddy's sister Helen recalls their local pastor coming to express condolences on behalf of the priests of the Creggan parish. 'I asked him where were the priests from the cathedral? I went to war on him, about one lot sneaking in the back door, saying they were sorry, and the other lot posting letters through the front door, condemning us. He just sat and took everything I said. Then a priest landed in from the cathedral. Fair play to him, he gave me the letter from the bishop, saying his only job was to deliver messages, and he asked me if he could wait while I read it. He was white as a sheet and pink with curiosity.' The RUC, waiting outside the front door, detained priests to ask them what was going on.

Sinn Féin was later to claim that the families were given to understand by mediators that requiem mass would be available, in the presence of the dead, in any church in Derry but the cathedral, where the bishop traditionally celebrated mass. The bishop is not aware of any such understanding. He was not in Derry during the final days of negotiation. He had left town to attend a weekend Youth Congress, fifteen miles away, in Strabane, which suffers the highest rate of unemployment in all of Europe.

Edward Daly does not know, nor wish to know, the

identity of the parishioners who gathered outside his home, in the precincts of the cathedral, asking him to change his edict. He has never looked, nor will he look, at media photographs of them. 'I don't want to know. I don't want anybody to think I bear them a grudge.'

His parishioners had come in the dark, on a wintry Friday night, in candle-lit procession. Their numbers, and the fact that the bishop had left town, encouraged Republicans to harden their demands in the names of the families. Since the dead men belonged to the cathedral parish, it was 'a matter of principle' that the remains should be brought there, and not to any other church, as mediators had indicated might be possible. Negotiations ended. It was a matter then of deciding exactly when the confrontation between the Church and the Republicans should take place and how it should proceed. It was agreed over the weekend that the funeral would begin on Monday morning. Nobody knew when the funeral would end, since the RUC was not a party to mediation.

*

On Sunday night Bishop Edward Daly left the country. He flew to London to observe on behalf of the Irish bishops, the political trial of the Birmingham Six, Irish immigrant men who denied that they had set off bombs in Birmingham which killed twenty-one people. Their alibi was that they had been travelling to Ireland at the time, to attend the funeral of a dead IRA man. The bishop's task, later that week, was to testify on their behalf and convince the highest court of appeal in Britain that many who attend IRA funerals do so out of respect and friendship for the dead person, and not because of any connection with, or support for, the IRA.

Bishop Edward Daly spent much of Monday morning ringing home constantly from a public phone in the court foyer. The phone in the presbytery in Derry was not always answered. The priests were outside looking upon a scene without precedent. Thousands of people had come marching into the grounds and up to the doors of the church, escorting the tricolour-draped coffins of Paddy Deery and Eddie McSheffrey. Fr Neil McGoldrick faced them and read out a statement which had been prepared over the weekend.

> I must register a protest at the entry of these funerals into the Cathedral against the express wishes of the Church authorities. To avoid any unbecoming scenes I have been advised by the Bishop to celebrate Requiem Mass forthwith.

Outright victory was not entirely with the Republicans, nor had they sought it. The day of interment had been chosen through negotiation and agreement because on that date, 2 November, since time immemorial, requiem mass has been said as a matter of course in every Catholic church in the world for the repose of all the souls of all the Catholics who have ever died.

It could not be said that Fr Michael Canney had been forced to say a requiem mass specifically for the souls of Paddy Deery and Eddie McSheffrey. His homily was graceful. 'At this time of year we think of those who have gone before us. Death, whether the death of a young person, someone in old age, a sudden death or a long illness, always brings a sense of grief and sadness when someone we love has been taken from us.'

As the cortege left the church grounds, the widows carried the IRA insignia, berets and gloves, of their husbands, in their hands. The first mourners through the gates were batoned by the police. They had not gone through the exit specified by the RUC, and now the police insisted, by force of arms, that they do what the police tell them. Blood was shed. The mourners retreated back into church grounds and asked the priests to negotiate on their behalf with the police.

His imaginative evocation of the scene still makes Bishop Edward Daly smile. 'Can you picture it? The police and the army are sitting outside one gate, in Land Rovers, drawn two abreast in a one-way street facing uphill. The people dive out the other gate, heading downhill, and God knows where they're going next.'

Thousands of people milled about the cathedral grounds, not knowing what would happen next. Hour after hour passed. Peggy Deery sat, exhausted, on the window sill of the presbytery. Her bad foot was chafed and bleeding. Her twelve surviving children, and their spouses and companions, and her twenty-six grandchildren, mingled with the throngs. The hearses had been moved under the protective covering of the church porch.

'You talk about a day trying to get somebody buried,' says Colette. 'That day was unbelievable. The Provos were saying we shouldn't leave unless the RUC kept such and such a distance from the funerals, so many feet in front of the hearse, so many feet behind all the mourners. The RUC were saying we couldn't leave unless we went out a certain gate, and walked a certain route. The Provos wouldn't agree with the route. It was something to do with where they planned to fire the volley of shots. They had the IRA in position somehere, and the escape route was already planned. To tell you the truth, I don't know what was going on.'

Peggy became ill. She kept shaking her head and saying: 'This is terrible.' At noon her daughter Bridie gathered up the youngest grandchildren and took them home. At two o'clock, Peggy was brought to her sister Nellie's house, where she took a sedative, lay down on the sofa and fell sound asleep. Shortly after that Colette had a meeting with the Republicans, in the privacy of the pews within the church. They wanted to bring the two coffins into the church and keep them there, overnight.

'It made great political sense,' says their chief strategist. 'There had been television broadcasts at lunchtime of the police laying into the mourners. The local radio was giving half-hourly updates. People were arriving all the time to join us. The more the police kept us trapped in there, the more the Church and the other politicians would have been been forced to condemn them. We could see it ending up with all the forces of nationalism ranged for the first time since Bloody Sunday against the Brits and their soldiers and police.'

Colette consulted an uncle of Paddy. He gave it as his considered opinion that relatives of a deceased person were only entitled to custody of a corpse for six days. On the seventh day, the police were allowed by law to snatch and bury it, wherever it lay. Next day would be the seventh day. Colette was appalled. 'They would have come into the church. They would have taken Paddy. They might have hurt and injured the old people.' She told the Republicans that she didn't care how they did it, but she wanted Paddy buried this day, the sixth day.

The Republicans, for their part, had a failure of nerve. They did not accept the uncle's opinion; but if, by some uncontrollable circumstance, their stage-managed trial of strength should result in war within church grounds, the aftermath for them would be catastrophic. Should Edward Daly feel honour-bound to resign his bishopric in consequence of violence in the cathedral, the Republicans were in no doubt as to what would happen to them. They would be shunned. Absent though he was, Bishop Edward Daly's place in politics and in the hearts of his parishioners assured his final authority. The Republicans moved out of the church and the grounds that Monday and led the cortege along the route dictated by the police.

The crucial concession that police not flank the cortege allowed the IRA to fire a volley of shots. Enraged, the RUC rushed the mourners, their ranks now swollen to include people of all nationalist political persuasion and none except that of opposition to those police. One of the coffins was knocked to the ground, the bones of the mourners were broken by batons and plastic bullets, and the IRA volunteer who fired the volley was shielded and spirited away, as it was known he would be, by the thousands who knew that during the course of the funeral armed tribute would be paid somehow, somewhere, to Paddy Deery and Eddie McSheffrey, but not within the grounds of a Catholic church.

The Last Gift

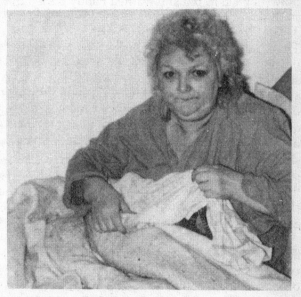

Peggy, two months before her death

When Peggy Deery woke up later that day, her son was long buried and the city was at peace. Peggy left her sister's house and went back up the hill to Creggan and went immediately to bed and the bed she lay in, virtually morning noon and night and all through the night, for the next three months, until she sickened unto her own death, was the bed of her other dead son Michael.

Owney's wife Donna wrote a poem for Peggy to console her about Paddy's death. It begins:

> Ah, congratulations, you are the proud parents of a baby son.
> Thank you nurses for all you have done.
> We took him home, full of joy,
> Our darling Paddy, baby boy.

They brought all their babies to her every Sunday afternoon, the twenty-six grandchildren and the twelve surviving children and their partners, crowding the house, crowding the bedroom, crowding out the past, trying to crowd the future with dreams of better days. A portable black-and-white TV set was installed at the foot of Peggy's bed. It was no use. Peggy was bleak.

One night Margie hit a royal flush on the poker machine in a city pub. She rang her mother and held the phone close to the machine that Peggy would hear the bells ring out, clocking up a one-hundred-pound pay-off. Life could yet yield windfalls. Peggy went back to bed.

Pio visited her mother every evening after Paddy died. 'If I just saw her out of bed, sitting in the kitchen, I thought it was great. The day she died, I'd gone up in the morning to the house. She was actually up, making the dinner. It was red fish and white sauce. I said, "Aren't you the grand one, up and about?" She said she was a wee bit sick, so I told her to go back to bed for a couple of hours. Margie and Kevin arrived and I went to the doctor's to get a wee abscess removed from the back of my neck. I went back up that night. She was in great form, silly and crazy and cracking jokes. Some of us were going to Buncrana to play the machines. She said why not play a hand of cards in the house "and if there's any money to be won, it'll be in the family". We said it wasn't the same. It wouldn't have been, all of us looking at one another and thinking. So some people stayed in the house with her, and off we went, Tony and me, and Tony's wife Lily, and May and Bess and Tony's mother-in-law. Tony stopped at Ballymagroarty on the way back. There was a priest standing outside my house. "I wonder what's up," I said. I had a wild feeling, I knew something bad had happened, but I never dreamt. All I remember now is the car speeding up to Creggan, Tony speeding away as he drove up the roads. We had to keep telling him to slow down. I wouldn't have cared if he crashed, but everybody else in the car was panicking. Tony said, "Fuck this. I can't believe it, what more's going to happen to us?"'

Her daughters heard Peggy call out before she died. June and Bernadette rushed upstairs and held their mother in their arms, and manoeuvred their mother onto the floor as she arched and scrambled and fought for breath. The neighbours and the doctor and Nellie came into the bedroom. 'Am I scaring you?' Peggy asked Bernadette, and Bernadette Devlin Deery bent to give her mother the kiss of life, and they kissed and Peggy Deery died then, on the night of 26 January 1988.

The only reading material in her bedroom was Paddy's memorial card, the verse of which she had chosen herself, and which she read constantly. It says:

Death is nothing at all. I have only slipped into the next room. Whatever we were to each, that we are still. Call me by my old familiar name, speak to me in the easy way which you always used. Laugh as we always laughed at the little jokes we enjoyed together. Pray, smile, think of me, pray for me. Let my name be the household word that it always was. Let it be spoken without effort. Life means all that it ever meant. It is the same as it ever was; there is absolutely unbroken continuity. Why should I be out of your sight? I am but waiting for you, for an interval, somewhere very near just around the corner. All is well. Nothing is past; nothing is lost. One brief moment and all will be as it was before – only better, infinitely happier and forever – we will all be one together with Christ. You, whom I have loved so much on earth, pray and live in such a manner that we may be re-united forever.

*

Peggy Deery was buried on a raw, wet, Friday morning. None of the mourners had a winter overcoat. The rain drenched them and left them sodden as they gathered round the open grave and prayed with the priest. When the priest left, Sinn Féin councillor Dodie McGuinness gave a brief oration. The rain-storm whipped her scarcely heard words away, carrying remnants of Peggy's life on the wind: '... civil rights ... Bloody Sunday ... house raided ... Paddy ...'

Sinn Féin had offered, and the family had accepted, a tricolour with which to cover Peggy's coffin during the funeral. There were no police or soldiers on the route, nor in the cemetery. There were no crowds. There was no trouble of any kind. There was just the family and friends. The tricolour was folded away and the family went home.

There they found Peggy's last gift to the children she considered gifts in her life. In her handbag were the hospital birth-tags of her twenty-six grandchildren, reassuring testimony that she loved them all, without exception or distinction, all of her children, and all of her children's children.

*

One month after Peggy's death, the family and relatives and neighbours gathered together in her living-room. The priest said mass there, praying for Peggy and Paddy and Michael. There was tea and sandwiches afterwards for the priest and the people. Her children reflected on their past and their future in wartime Derry. Helen said, 'I couldn't care less. I don't give a damn any more.' Pio considered moving across the border into Donegal, near her husband's people. 'I wouldn't move for the sake of being in some kind of free Ireland. A United Ireland or not doesn't really bother me. It's just that Derry's not the same now without me ma, and Paddy's gone, so the war's over for me. It makes you bitter. People say to me, "How can you still be bitter?" but it has to fall on you, to know the way it leaves you.' Johnny, who did not come for the mass, said, 'No matter what ever happened to me, my ma was always sent for. That's why I'm fucking lost without her. Like, if I was lifted and brought to prison, I always knew she'd be up to see me. We had a special relationship.'

*

The four daughters who were living with Peggy at the time of her death came to a gentle and natural agreement about where and how they should live now. June and Bernadette, the two youngest of Peggy's children, went with June's baby to live with Margie. May and Bess stayed on with May's baby in their mother's home.

These two young women, living with an infant in a house which once sheltered their twelve brothers and sisters and their mother as well, feel dislocated and isolated, though 82 Creggan Heights would be considered, in normal circumstances, a warm and snug place and merely adequate to their needs. 'It's like a big empty house,' says Bess. 'You can hear yourself flying around in it.' The rest of the family call in now at all hours to keep them company, to keep the tradition of unity going.

Tony and his wife Lily, living a few doors away, stop in on their way home to bed. The soldiers taunt Tony about the silvery trousers he always wears when he dresses up. They belonged to Paddy, who bought them just before he died. Margie, especially, pays visits, checking the rent book and the electricity bills and the phone bill, and the housekeeping money which May and Bess keep in a jar. Every Sunday, just as their mother did, May and Bess send a cooked dinner, in a pot, down to Aunt Nellie. The gravy is put in a separate vessel which is covered with clingfilm, just as their mother covered it. Every night before she goes to sleep, Aunt Nellie rings up to say: 'God bless.'

Glossary

Anglo-Irish Agreement — The Anglo-Irish Agreement was signed between Britain and the Republic of Ireland in November 1985 and lodged as an international treaty. It established a consultative role for the government of the Republic in the administration of Northern Irish affairs, closer security co-operation and extradition from the Republic to Northern Ireland and Britain. In signing the agreement, the Republic officially recognised the Northern Irish state for the first time and the British state conceded that the political status of Northern Ireland in the future would be determined by a majority vote. The agreement is subject to review. It is the first attempt to move outside an exclusively Northern Irish framework since the Sunningdale Agreement but has brought little promised reform in the administration of justice in Northern Ireland. The emphasis to date has been almost exclusively on 'security'.

Civil Rights Movement — Inspired by the black Civil Rights Movement in America, the Northern Ireland Civil Rights Movement emerged in 1967 united around demands for 'one man — one vote' and equal access to housing and jobs for Catholics and Protestants. It was the most successful, broad-based mass campaign against the sectarian nature of the Northern Irish state and drew significant Protestant as well as Catholic support. It was the extreme and violent response by the Northern Irish security forces against the peaceful civil rights marches which first brought Northern Ireland to international attention.

Direct Rule — Up until 1972, Northern Ireland was administered by the Unionist controlled parliament based in Stormont Castle. Civil unrest and mass opposition to the sectarian administration led to the fall of Stormont and 'direct rule' was imposed from Westminster, integrating the day-to-day administration of Northern Ireland into the British state. In 1974 the British Conservative Government signed the Sunningdale Agreement establishing a Council of Ireland and a power-sharing executive. This guaranteed Catholic representation in the administration. Unionists' opposition to the agreement was vehement, culminating in the Ulster Workers' Council strike which paralysed the Northern Irish state. As a result, the British abandoned the agreement and direct rule continued.

Emergency Provisions Act 1973 — Northern Ireland has been in a 'state of emergency' since the inception of the State in 1922. The Emergency Provisions Act 1973 replaced the Special Powers Act 1922 as the British administration reorganised the legislative framework of Northern Ireland. This act gives the army and police sweeping powers of arrest, search and detention, and abolished the 'right to silence'. It suspends the basic civil liberties of anyone 'suspected of being a terrorist', in situations where no charges have yet, or may ever, be preferred.

Gerrymander — A popular term used to describe vote rigging in Northern Ireland, where constituency boundaries were drawn in such a way as to ensure that the Catholic population had significantly fewer public representatives than their numbers warranted. In Derry and Fermanagh, for example, where Catholics outnumbered Protestants, Protestants were enabled to return the majority of representatives.

Housing Executive — Housing has always been one of the most visible areas of discrimination against Catholics in Northern Ireland. The Housing Executive was set up in 1971 to remove housing allocation from the direct control of largely Unionist controlled local authorities.

Internment — Internment, a policy of mass imprisonment without trial, has been recurrently used against the Republican movement in both Northern Ireland and the Republic since partition. In August 1971, dawn swoops saw thousands of Catholics detained in barbed-wire compounds, denied the most basic civil rights and subjected to brutal and humiliating treatment.

IRA — The Irish Republican Army has been in existence for nearly one hundred years, carrying out successive military campaigns against British rule in Ireland. Although policies have varied over the years and the organisation has split on a number of occasions, the IRA, together with the political organisation Sinn Féin, maintains the demand for British withdrawal and a belief that British imperialism will not disengage from Northern Ireland unless forced to. The IRA is a proscribed organisation in both Northern Ireland and the Republic, where a membership charge carries a sentence of seven years imprisonment.

Payment for Debt Act, 1971 — As a protest against internment, the Catholic population went on rent and rates strike in 1971, withholding payments from public bodies. In response the Payment for Debt (Emergency Provisions) Act 1971, a repressive emergency law, was introduced. This Act allows the state to deduct at source from people's welfare payments where they are in arrears to public agencies. Its aim is to make such acts of civil disobedience financially impossible. In 1974, the Catholic leadership which called originally for the rent strike, called it off in exchange for ministries, under the Sunningdale Agreement. Internment continued.

Poppy Day/Remembrance Sunday — This is the date on which the armistice was signed at the end of the First World War and is a day set aside by the British and the Commonwealth to commemorate the dead of the First and Second World Wars, marked by ceremonies and the wearing of a red poppy. In Northern Ireland, the occasion is marked by Unionist supremacy, a day when Catholics remain indoors.

Strip Searching — Strip searching is a policy pursued by the British administration designed to humiliate and demoralise Republican prisoners, particularly those 'on remand' whose trials have yet to be completed. It was introduced ostensibly for 'security reasons' but involves the systematic and forced stripping and searching of prisoners in the presence of a group of prison officers, as often as a dozen times in a single day. Journeys to and from court hearings are particularly used for this purpose. Women Republican prisoners have been specially targeted by this policy which amounts to a form of sexual harassment.

Unionist — Unionists hold the political position ·that Northern Ireland should remain part of the United Kingdom, *i.e.* the union with Britain should be maintained. Unionism controlled Stormont, the

Northern Irish parliament, from its birth in 1922 until it collapsed in 1972, guaranteeing a position of power and/or privilege to its, almost exclusively, Protestant adherents. The Unionist power block splintered as Northern Ireland became engulfed in crisis: the Official Unionist Party now represents upper- and middle-class Protestants while the Democratic Unionist Party (led by Rev. Ian Paisley) takes a more militant fundamentalist stance, drawing on substantial Protestant working-class support.

UVF — The Ulster Volunteer Force is a proscribed military organisation dedicated to the maintenance of the Protestant ascendency. It engages in both sectarian attacks against the Catholic population and retaliatory actions against the Republican movement.

Chronology

Chronology of Events

October 5 1968: First civil rights march in Derry. Peggy Deery takes part.

November 1968: Derry Corporation abolished.

April 1969: First civilian death in North. Sam Devenney dies in Derry of baton wounds from RUC.

August 15 1969: British troops deployed in the North.

March 3 1971: First British soldier killed in Derry.

May 18 1971: Peggy's last and fourteenth child born.

July 8 1971: First civilian killed by soldiers in Derry.

August 9 1971: Internment introduced in North. Nationalists go on rent and rate strike. Payment for Debt Act introduced.

August 18 1971: First IRA volunteer killed in Derry.

October 5 1971: Peggy's husband dies.

January 31 1972: Bloody Sunday in Derry. Soldiers kill 13 people and wound 28, including Peggy Deery.

March 24 1972: Edward Heath abolishes Stormont government. Direct rule introduced.

August 9 1972: Peggy's son Paddy partially blinded by soldiers.

1972: Dublin introduces anti-IRA emergency legislation.

January 1974: Heath establishes Power-sharing Executive in North under Sunningdale agreement.

March 1974: Labour returned under Wilson.

May 14 1974: Loyalist workers strike against Sunningdale Executive.

May 17 1974: Loyalist bombs kill 29 in Republic of Ireland.

May 28 1974: Executive collapses. Direct rule resumed.

1975: Internment ended.

1976: Prevention of Terrorism Act introduced to North and to Britain.

1981: Ten IRA men die of hunger strike in prison in North.

1983: Dublin government introduces constitutional prohibition of abortion.

November 1985: Anglo-Irish Security Agreement is signed by Margaret Thatcher and Garret FitzGerald.

1986: Referendum confirms prohibition on divorce in the Republic of Ireland.

March 13 1986: Peggy's son Michael is killed.

October 28 1987: Peggy's son Paddy is killed.

December 1987: Dublin passes Bill to extradite members of the IRA to Northern Ireland.

January 28 1988: Peggy dies.